Anecdotes
Incidents *and* Illustrations

BY

D. L. Moody.

THE MOODY PRESS

CHICAGO

Printed in the United States of America

PREFACE

When I was preaching in Baltimore in 1879, an infidel reporter, who believed I was a humbug, came to the meetings with the express purpose of catching me in my remarks. He believed that my stories and anecdotes were all made up, and he intended to expose me in his paper.

One of the anecdotes I told was as follows:

A gentleman was walking down the streets of a city some time before. It was near Christmas-time, and many of the shop windows were filled with Christmas presents and toys. As this gentleman passed along, he saw three little girls standing before a shop window. Two of them were trying to describe to the third the things that were in the window. It aroused his attention, and he wondered what it could mean. He went back, and found that the middle one was blind—she had never been able to see—and her two sisters were endeavoring to tell her how the things looked. The gentleman stood beside them for some time and listened; he said it was most interesting to hear them trying to describe the different articles to the blind child—they found it a difficult task.

"That is just my position in trying to tell other men about Christ," I said; "I may talk about Him; and yet they see no beauty in Him that they should desire Him.

But if they will only come to Him, He will open their eyes and reveal Himself to them in all His loveliness and grace."

After the meeting this reporter came to me and asked where I got that story. I said I had read it in a Boston paper. He told me that it had happened right there in the streets of Baltimore, and that he was the gentleman referred to! It made such an impression on him that he accepted Christ and became one of the first converts in that city.

Many and many a time I have found that when the sermon—and even the text—has been forgotten, some story has fastened itself in a hearer's mind, and has borne fruit. Anecdotes are like windows to let light in upon a subject. They have a useful ministry, and I pray God to bless this collection to every reader.

D. L. Moody.

ANECDOTES, INCIDENTS AND ILLUSTRATIONS

Wanted—A New Song!

There was a Wesleyan preacher in England, Peter Mackenzie, full of native humor, a most godly man. He was once preaching from the text: "And They Sang a New Song," and he said:

"Yes, there will be singing in heaven, and when I get there I will want to have David with his harp, and Paul, and Peter and other saints gather around for a sing. And I will announce a hymn from the Wesleyan Hymnal. 'Let us sing hymn No. 749—'

> My God, my Father, while I stray—

"But some one will say, 'That won't do. You are in heaven, Peter; there's no straying here.' And I will say, 'Yes, that's so. Let us sing No. 651—'

> Though waves and storms go o'er my head,
> Though friends be gone and hopes be dead—

"But another saint will interrupt, 'Peter, you forget you are in heaven now; there are no storms here.' 'Well, I will try again, No. 536—'

> Into a world of ruffians sent—

"'Peter! Peter!' some one will say, 'we will put you out unless you stop giving out inappropriate hymns.' I will ask—what can we sing? And they will all say:

"'Sing the new song, the song of Moses and the Lamb.'"

Nothing to Hold On To

It is related of an atheist who was dying that he appeared very uncomfortable, very unhappy and frightened. Another atheist who stood at his bedside said to him:

"Don't be afraid. Hold on, man, hold on to the last."

The dying man said: "That is what I want to do, but tell me what to hold on to?"

What Could the King Do?

In the second century they brought a Christian before a king, who wanted him to recant and give up Christ and Christianity, but the man spurned the proposition. But the king said:

"If you don't do it, I will banish you."

The man smiled and answered, "You can't banish me from Christ, for He says He will never leave me nor forsake me."

The king got angry, and said: "Well, I will confiscate your property and take it all from you."

And the man replied: "My treasures are laid up on high; you cannot get them."

The king became still more angry, and said: "I will kill you."

"Why," the man answered, "I have been dead forty years; I have been dead with Christ, dead to the world, and my life is hid with Christ in God, and you cannot touch it."

"What are you going to do with such a fanatic?" said the king.

Always Praising

A man was converted some years ago, and he was just full of praise. He was living in the light all the time. He used to preface everything he said in the meeting with "Praise God!"

One night he came to the meeting with his finger all bound up. He had cut it, and cut it pretty bad, too. Well, I wondered how he would praise God for this; but he got up and said:

"I have cut my finger, but, praise God, I didn't cut it off!"

If things go against you, just remember they might be a good deal worse.

Not at all Absurd

A man said to me some time ago, "Moody, the doctrine you preach is most absurd: you preach that men have only to *believe* to change the whole course of their life. A man will not change his course by simply believing."

I said—"I think I can make you believe that in less than two minutes."

"No, you can't," he said; "I'll never believe it."

I said, "Let us make sure that we understand each other. You say a man is not affected by what he believes, that it will not change the course of his actions?"

"I do."

"Supposing," I said, "a man should put his head in at that door and say the house was on fire, what would you do? You would get out by the window if you believed it, wouldn't you?"

"Oh," he replied, "I didn't think of that!"

"No," I said, "I guess you didn't."

Belief is the foundation of all society, of commerce, and of everything else.

Not Too Great for Cæsar

It is said that on one occasion when Cæsar gave a very valuable present, the receiver replied that it was too costly a gift. The Emperor answered that it was not too great for Cæsar to give.

Our God is a great King, and He delights to give gifts to us: so let us delight to ask Him for great things.

A Good Samaritan

I remember the first good Samaritan I ever saw. I had been in this world only three or four years when my father died a bankrupt, and the creditors came and swept away about everything we had. My widow mother had a cow and a few things, and it was a hard struggle to keep the wolf from the door. My brother went to Greenfield, and secured work in a store for his board, and went to school. It was so lonely there that he wanted me to get a place so as to be with him, but I didn't want to leave home. One cold day in November my brother came home and said he had a place for me. I said that I wouldn't go, but after it was talked over they decided I should go. I didn't want my brothers to know that I hadn't the courage to go, but that night was a long one.

The next morning we started. We went up on the hill, and had a last sight of the old house. We sat down there and cried. I thought that would be the last time I should ever see that old home. I cried all the way down to Greenfield. There my brother introduced me to an old man who was so old he couldn't milk his cows and do the chores, so I was to do his errands, milk his cows and go to school. I looked at the old man and saw he was cross. I took a good look at the wife and thought she was crosser than the old man. I stayed there an hour and it seemed like a week. I went around then to my brother and said:

"I am going home."

"What are you going home for?"

"I am homesick," I said.

"Oh well, you will get over it in a few days."

"I never will," I said. "I don't want to."

He said, "You will get lost if you start for home now; it is getting dark."

I was frightened then, as I was only about ten years old, and I said, "I will go at daybreak to-morrow morning."

He took me to a shop window, where they had some jackknives and other things, and tried to divert my mind. What did I care for those old jackknives? I wanted to get back home to my mother and brothers; it seemed as if my heart was breaking.

All at once my brother said, "Dwight, there comes a man that will give you a cent."

"How do you know he will?" I asked.

"Oh! he gives every new boy that comes to town a cent."

I brushed away the tears, for I wouldn't have him see me crying, and I got right in the middle of the sidewalk, where he couldn't help but see me, and kept my eyes right upon him. I remember how that old man looked as he came tottering down the sidewalk. Oh, such a bright, cheerful, sunny face he had! When he came opposite to where I was he stopped, took my hat off, put his hand on my head, and said to my brother:

"This is a new boy in town, isn't it?"

"Yes, sir, he is; just came to-day."

I watched to see if he would put his hand into his

pocket. I was thinking of that cent. He began to talk to me so kindly that I forgot all about it. He told me that God had an only Son, and He sent Him down here, and wicked men killed Him, and he said He died for me. He only talked five minutes, but he took me captive. After he had given me this little talk, he put his hand in his pocket and took out a brand new cent, a copper that looked just like gold. He gave me that; I thought it was gold, and didn't I hold it tight! I never felt so rich before or since. I don't know what became of that cent; I have always regretted that I didn't keep it; but I can feel the pressure of the old man's hand on my head to-day. Fifty years have rolled away, and I can hear those kind words ringing yet. I never shall forget that act. He put the money at usury; that cent has cost me a great many dollars. I have never walked up the streets of this country or the old country but down into my pocket goes my hand, and I take out some money and give it to every forlorn, miserable child I see. I think how the old man lifted a load from me, and I want to lift a load from some one else.

Do you want to be like Christ? Go and find some one who has fallen, and get your arm under him, and lift him up toward heaven. The Lord will bless you in the very act. May God help us to go and do like the good Samaritan!

Covetous Till Death

An English clergyman was called to the death-bed of a wealthy parishioner. Kneeling beside the dying man the pastor asked him to take his hand as he prayed for his upholding in that solemn hour, but he declined to give it. After the end had come, and they turned down the coverlet, the rigid hands were found holding the safe-key in their death-grip. Heart and hand, to the last, clinging to his possessions, but he could not take them with him.

He Had his Eyes Opened

The story is told of a boy whose parents took him to Florida to spend the winter. He returned to his city home, disgusted with the country he had been in. It was dull, stupid, and uninteresting, he said. During the next few months, however, he was in charge of a tutor who was an enthusiastic botanist, and he kindled the boy's interest in his favorite study. The boy learned about orchids, and their strange life. His tutor took him to a conservatory that he might see some of them growing.

"You should see them in Florida," the tutor said, "they are much better there; but these will give you an idea."

The boy looked at him in amazement.

"I have been in Florida," he said, "but I never noticed any of them."

"Perhaps you did not look for them," the tutor answered; "but they will not escape you the next time."

That is often the way with the Bible. A person sees no beauty in it, but the Holy Spirit is ready to open the eyes of our understanding and teach us. It may be by some sermon or book which will lift a truth out of its hiding-place, and give it an application to our life it never had before.

A True Proverb

An Arab proverb runs thus: "The neck is bent by the sword, but heart is only bent by heart." **Love is irresistible.**

Are *You* Seeking Rest?

A lady in Wales told me this little story: An English friend of hers, a mother, had a child that was sick. At first they considered there was no danger, until one day the doctor came in and said that the symptoms were very unfavorable. He took the mother out of the room, and told her that the child could not live. It came like a thunderbolt. After the doctor had gone the mother went into the room where the child lay and began to talk to the child, and tried to divert its mind.

"Darling, do you know you will soon hear the music of heaven? You will hear a sweeter song than you have ever heard on earth. You will hear them sing the song of Moses and the Lamb. You are very fond of music. Won't it be sweet, darling?"

And the little tired, sick child turned its head away, and said, "Oh, mamma, I am so tired and so sick that I think it would make me worse to hear all that music."

"Well," the mother said, "you will soon see Jesus. You will see the seraphim and cherubim and the streets all paved with gold"; and she went on picturing heaven as it is described in Revelation.

The little tired child again turned its head away, and said, "Oh, mamma, I am so tired that I think it would make me worse to see all those beautiful things!"

At last the mother took the child up in her arms, and pressed her to her loving heart. And the little sick one whispered:

"Oh, mamma, that is what I want. If Jesus will only take me in His arms and let me rest!"

Dear friend, are you not tired and weary of sin? **Are you** not weary of the turmoil of life? You can find **rest** on the bosom of the Son of God.

Humility

Some years ago I saw what is called a sensitive plant. I happened to breathe on it, and suddenly it drooped its head; I touched it, and it withered away. Humility is as sensitive as that; it cannot safely be brought out on exhibition. A man who is flattering himself that he is humble and is walking close to the Master, is self-deceived. It consists not in thinking meanly of ourselves, but in not thinking of ourselves at all. Moses wist not that his face shone. If humility speaks of itself, it is gone.

A New Man in Old Clothes

A man got up in one of our meetings in New York some years ago, who had been pretty far down, but a wonderful change had taken place, and he said he hardly knew himself. He said the fact was, he was a new man in his old clothes.

That was just it. Not a man in new clothes, but a new man in old clothes.

I saw an advertisement which read like this: "If you want people to respect you, wear good clothes." That is the world's idea of getting the world's respect. Why! A leper may put on good clothes, but he is a leper still. Mere profession doesn't transform a man. It is the new nature spoken of in 2d Corinthians, 5th chapter, 17th verse, "Therefore if any man be in Christ, he is a new creature; old things are passed away; behold, all things are become new."

Proud of Their False Religions

I do not believe there is any false religion in the world that men are not proud of. The only religion of which I have ever heard, that men were ashamed of, is the religion of Jesus Christ. Some time ago I preached two weeks in Salt Lake City, and I did not find a Mormon that was not proud of his religion. When I came within forty miles of Salt Lake City, the engineer came into the car and wanted to know if I wouldn't like to ride on the engine. I went with him, and in that forty mile ride he talked Mormonism to me the whole time, and tried to convert me so that I would not preach against the Mormons. I never met an unconverted Chinaman who wasn't proud of being a disciple of Confucius; and I never met a Mohammedan who wasn't proud of the fact that he was a follower of Mohammed; but how many, many times I have found men ashamed of the religion of Jesus Christ, the only religion that gives men the power over their affections and lusts and sins. If there was some back-door by which men could slip into heaven, there would be a great many who would want to enter it, but they don't like to make public confession.

This is Our Hope

A bright young girl of fifteen was suddenly cast upon a bed of suffering, completely paralyzed on one side and nearly blind. She heard the family doctor say to her parents as they stood by the bedside—

"She has seen her best days, poor child!"

"No, doctor," she exclaimed, "my best days are yet to come, when I shall see the King in His beauty."

That is our hope. We shall not sink into annihilation. Christ rose from the dead to give us a pledge of our own rising. The resurrection is the great antidote for fear of death. Nothing else can take its place. Riches, genius, worldly pleasures or pursuits, none can bring us consolation in the dying hour. "All my possessions for a moment of time," cried Queen Elizabeth, when dying. "I have provided in the course of my life for everything except death, and now, alas! I am to die unprepared," were the last words of Cardinal Borgia. Compare with these the last words of one of the early disciples: "I am weary. I will now go to sleep. Good night!" He had the sure hope of awaking in a brighter land.

The Blind Man and the Lantern

I remember reading of a blind man who was found sitting at the corner of a street in a great city with a lantern beside him. Some one went up to him and asked what he had the lantern there for, seeing that he was blind, and the light was the same to him as the darkness. The blind man replied:

"I have it so that no one may stumble over me."

Dear friends, let us think of that. Where one man reads the Bible, a hundred read you and me. That is what Paul meant when he said we were to be "living epistles of Christ, known and read of all men." I would not give much for all that can be done by sermons, if we do not preach Christ by our lives. If we do not commend the Gospel to people by our holy walk and conversation, we shall not win them to Christ.

How Prophecy is Fulfilled

Dr. Cyrus Hamlin tells the following story. While he was in Constantinople soon after the Crimean War, a colonel in the Turkish army called to see him, and said:

"I want to ask you one question. What proof can you give me that the Bible is what you claim it to be—the word of God?"

Dr. Hamlin evaded the question, and drew him into

conversation, during which he learned that his visitor had traveled a great deal, especially in the East in the region of the Euphrates.

"Were you ever in Babylon?" asked the doctor.

"Yes, and that reminds me of a curious experience I had there. I am very fond of sport, and having heard that the ruins of Babylon abound in game, I determined to go there for a week's shooting. Knowing that it was not considered safe for a man to be there except in the company of several others—and money being no object to me—I engaged a sheik with his followers to accompany me for a large sum. We reached Babylon and pitched our tents. A little before sundown I took my gun and strolled out to have a look around. The holes and caverns among the mounds which cover the ruins are infested with game, which, however, is rarely seen except at night. I caught sight of one or two animals in the distance, and then turned my steps toward our encampment, intending to begin my sport as soon as the sun had set. What was my surprise to find the men striking the tents! I went to the sheik and protested most strongly. I had engaged him for a week, and was paying him handsomely, and here he was starting off before our contract had scarcely begun. Nothing I could say, however, would induce him to remain. 'It isn't safe,' he said. 'No mortal flesh dare stay here after sunset. In the dark ghosts, goblins, ghouls, and all sorts of things come out of the holes and caverns and whoever is found here is taken off by them and becomes one of themselves.' Finding that I could not persuade him, I said, 'Well, as it is I'm paying you more than I ought to, but if you'll stay I'll double it.' 'No,' he said, 'I couldn't stay for all the money in the world. No Arab has ever seen the sun go down on Babylon. But I want to do what is right by you. We'll go off to a place about an hour distant and come back at daybreak.' And go they did. And my sport had to be given up."

"As soon as he had finished," said Dr. Hamlin, "I took my Bible and read from it the 13th chapter of Isaiah: 'And Babylon, the glory of kingdoms, the beauty of the Chaldees' excellency, shall be as when God overthrew Sodom and Gomorrah. It shall never be inhabited, neither shall it be dwelt in from generation to generation; neither shall the Arabian pitch tent there; neither shall the shepherds make their fold there: but wild beasts of the desert shall lie there: and their houses shall be full of doleful creatures: and owls shall dwell there, and satyrs shall dance there. And the wild beasts of the islands shall cry in their desolate houses, and dragons in their pleasant palaces: and her time is near to come, and her days shall not be prolonged.'"

"That's it exactly," said the Turk when I had finished, "but that's history you've been reading."

"No," answered Dr. Hamlin, "it's prophecy. Come, you're an educated man. You know that the Old Testament was translated into Greek about three hundred years before Christ." He acknowledged that it was. "And the Hebrew was given at least two hundred years before that?" "Yes." "Well, wasn't this written when Babylon was in its glory, and isn't it prophecy?"

"I'm not prepared to give you an answer now," he replied. "I must have time to think it over."

"Very well, ' Dr. Hamlin said, "Do so, and come back when you're ready and give me your answer."

From that day to this he had never seen him, but what an unexpected testimony to the truth of the Bible in regard to the fulfillment of prophecy did that Turkish officer give!

The Devil Knew He Could Wait

There is a story of an old Christian slave in the South whose master was an infidel. One day the master went duck-shooting with his slave, and turning on him suddenly, he said:

"How is it, uncle, that the devil never tempts me, and always worries you? Why should he tempt a Christian more than an infidel?"

Before the slave could find an answer, a flock of ducks came within range and the master fired into them. He then directed the slave to make haste to secure the wounded birds first, and let those that were dead wait till last. When the slave returned to his master he had found his answer:

"You see, massa, I reckon it is this way about the devil. He thinks I'm only a poor, wounded soul that he wants to make sure of first, but you are surely his, and so you can wait."

There was a great deal of theology in the old man's reasoning. When a man is truly born of God, it seems as if every influence of evil is arrayed against him, and unless the work is genuine he will not stand. I know of a certain temperance lecturer who was once a poor, wretched drunkard. A short time after his conversion he was asked to speak in his native town, and when he came on the stage it was found that liquor had been sprinkled about the floor in order that its fumes might tempt him to drink again.

That Ladder a Dream

A man dreamt that he built a ladder from earth to heaven, and when he did a good deed up went his ladder a few feet. When he did a very good deed his ladder went higher, and when he gave away large sums of money to the poor up it went further still. By and by it went out of sight, and as years rolled on, it went up, he thought, past the clouds, clear into heaven. When he died he thought he would step off his ladder into heaven, but he heard a voice roll out from paradise:

"He that climbeth up some other way, the same is a thief and a robber."

Down he came, ladder and all, and he awoke. He said if he wanted to get salvation he must get it in another way than by good deeds, and he took the other way, which is by Jesus Christ.

The Arrow Hit the Mark

A society was some years ago established to distribute tracts by mail in the higher circles. One of these tracts, entitled, "Prepare to meet thy God," was enclosed in an envelope, and sent by post to a gentleman well known for his ungodly life and his reckless impiety. He was in his study when he read this letter among others.

"What's that?" said he. "'Prepare to meet thy God.' Who has had the impudence to send me this cant?" And, with an imprecation on his unknown correspondent, he arose to put the paper in the fire.

"No; I won't do that," he said to himself. "On second thoughts, I know what I will do. I'll send it to my friend B——; it will be a good joke to hear what he'll say about it."

So saying, he enclosed the tract in a fresh envelope,

and in a feigned hand directed it to his boon companion.

Mr. B—— was a man of his own stamp, and received the tract, as his friend had done, with an oath at the Methodist humbug; and his first impulse was to tear in pieces. "I'll not tear it either," said he to himself. "Prepare to meet thy God" at once arrested his attention and smote his conscience. The arrow of conviction entered his heart as he read, and he was converted.

Almost his first thought was for his ungodly associates. "Have I received such blessed light and truth, and shall I not strive to communicate it to others?" He again folded the tract, and enclosed and directed it to one of his companions in sin. Wonderful to say, the little arrow hit the mark. His friend read. He also was converted; and both are now walking as the Lord's redeemed ones.

Is There Anything to Cultivate?

We hear nowadays so much about "culture." Culture's all right when you have something to cultivate. If 1 should plant a watch, I shouldn't get any little watches, would I? Why? Because the seed of life is not there. But let me plant some peas or potatoes, and I will get a crop.

Don't let any man or woman rest short of being born of the Spirit of God. First make sure that you have that divine nature, then cultivate it.

For Parents

Whenever I speak to parents, two fathers come before me. One lived on the Mississippi River. He was a man of great wealth. One day his eldest boy had been borne home unconscious. They did everything that man could do to restore him, but in vain. Time passed, and after a terrible suspense he recovered consciousness.

"My son," the father whispered, "the doctor tells me you are dying."

"Oh!" said the boy, "you never prayed for me, father; won't you pray for my lost soul now?"

The father wept. It was true he had never prayed. He was a stranger to God. And in a little while that soul, unprayed for, passed into its dark eternity.

The father has since said that he would give all his wealth if he could call back his boy only to offer one short prayer for him.

What a contrast is the other father! He, too, had a lovely son, and one day he came home to find him at the gates of death. His wife was weeping, and she said:

"Our boy is dying; he has had a change for the worse. I wish you would go in and see him."

The father went into the room and placed his hand upon the brow of his dying boy, and could feel the cold, damp sweat was gathering there; the cold, icy hand of death was feeling for the chords of life.

"Do you know, my son, that you are dying?" asked the father.

"Am I? Is this death? Do you really think I am dying?"

"Yes, my son, your end on earth is near."

"And will I be with Jesus tonight, father?"

"Yes, you will soon be with the Savior."

"Father, don't weep, for when I get there I will go straight to Jesus and tell him that you have been trying all my life to lead me to Him."

God has given me three children, and ever since I can remember I have directed them to Christ. I would rather they carried this message to Jesus—that I had tried all their life to lead them to Him—than have all the crowns of the earth; I would rather lead them to Jesus than give them the wealth of the world.

How I Came to Give Up Business

The way God led me out of business into Christian work was as follows:

I had never lost sight of Jesus Christ since the first night I met Him in the store at Boston. But for years I was only a nominal Christian, really believing that I could not work for God. No one had ever asked me to do anything.

When I went to Chicago, I hired five pews in a church, and used to go out on the street, and pick up young men, and fill these pews. I never spoke to those young men about their souls; that was the work of the elders, I thought. After working for some time like that, I started a mission Sabbath school. I thought numbers were everything, and so I worked for numbers. When the attendance ran below one thousand, it troubled me; and when it ran to twelve or fifteen hundred, I was elated. Still none were converted; there was no harvest. Then God opened my eyes.

There was a class of young ladies in the school, who were without exception the most frivolous set of girls I ever met. One Sunday the teacher was ill, and I took that class. They laughed in my face, and I felt like opening the door and telling them all to get out and never come back.

That week the teacher of the class came into the store where I worked. He was pale, and looked very ill.

"What is the trouble?" I asked.

"I have had another hemorrhage of my lungs. The doctor says I cannot live on Lake Michigan, so I am going to New York State. I suppose I am going home to die."

He seemed greatly troubled, and when I asked him the reason, he replied:

"Well, I have never led any of my class to Christ. I really believe I have done the girls more harm than good."

I had never heard any one talk like that before, and it set me thinking.

After a while I said: "Suppose you go and tell them how you feel. I will go with you in a carriage, if you want to go."

He consented, and we started out together. It was one of the best journeys I ever had on earth. We went to the house of one of the girls, called for her, and the teacher talked to her about her soul. There was no laughing then! Tears stood in her eyes before long. After he had explained the way of life, he suggested that we have prayer. He asked me to pray. True, I had never done such a thing in my life as to pray God to convert a young lady there and then. But we prayed, and God answered our prayer.

We went to other houses. He would go upstairs, and be all out of breath, and he would tell the girls what he had come for. It wasn't long before they broke down, and sought salvation.

When his strength gave out, I took him back to his lodgings. The next day we went out again. At the end of ten days he came to the store with his face literally shining.

"Mr. Moody," he said, "the last one of my class has yielded herself to Christ."

I tell you, we had a time of rejoicing.

He had to leave the next night, so I called his class together that night for a prayer-meeting, and there God kindled a fire in my soul that has never gone out. The height of my ambition had been to be a successful merchant, and if I had known that meeting was going to take that ambition out of me, I might not have gone. But how many times I have thanked God since for that meeting!

The dying teacher sat in the midst of his class, and talked with them, and read the 14th chapter of John. We tried to sing "Blest be the tie that binds," after which we knelt down to prayer. I was just rising from my knees, when one of the class began to pray for her dying teacher. Another prayed, and another, and before we rose, the whole class had prayed. As I went out I said to myself:

"Oh, God, let me die rather than lose the blessing I have received to-night!"

The next evening I went to the depot to say good-bye to that teacher. Just before the train started, one of the class came, and before long, without any prearrangement, they were all there. What a meeting that was! We tried to sing, but we broke down. The last we saw of that dying teacher, he was standing on the platform of the car, his finger pointing upward, telling that class to meet him in heaven.

I didn't know what this was going to cost me. I was disqualified for business; it had become distasteful to me. I had got a taste of another world, and cared no more for making money. For some days after, the greatest struggle of my life took place. Should I give up business and give myself to Christian work, or should I not? I have never regretted my choice. Oh, the luxury of leading some one out of the darkness of this world into the glorious light and liberty of the Gospel!

"Mind Your Own Business!"

One night in Chicago, many years ago, when I was on my way home I saw a man leaning against a lamppost. Stepping up to him and placing my hand on his shoulder, I said:

"Are you a Christian?"

The man flew into a rage, doubled up his fist and I thought he was going to pitch me into the gutter.

I said: "I'm very sorry if I've offended you, but I thought I was asking a proper question."

"Mind your own business," he roared.

"That is my business," I answered.

About three months later, on a bitter cold morning about daybreak, some one knocked at my door.

"Who's there!" I asked.

A stranger answered, and I said: "What do you want?"

"I want to become a Christian," was the reply.

I opened the door, and to my astonishment there was the man who had cursed me for talking to him as he leaned against the lamppost.

He said: "I'm very sorry. I haven't had any peace since that night. Your words have haunted and troubled me. I couldn't sleep last night, and I thought I'd come and get you to pray for me."

That man accepted Christ, and the moment he had done so, asked:

"What can I do for Him?"

He taught in the Sabbath school until the war broke out, when he enlisted, and was one of the first to be shot down, but not before he had given a ringing testimony for God.

The Others Were Sorry

A Sunday school teacher wished to show his class how free the gift of God is. He took a silver watch from his pocket and offered it to the eldest boy in the class.

"It's yours, if you will take it."

The little fellow sat and grinned at the teacher. He thought he was joking. The teacher offered it to the next boy, and said:

"Take that watch: it is yours."

The little fellow thought he would be laughed at if he held out his hand, and therefore he sat still. In the same way the teacher went nearly round the class; but not one of them would accept the proffered gift. At length he came to the smallest boy. When the watch was offered to the little fellow, he took it and put it into his pocket. All the class laughed at him.

"I am thankful, my boy," said the teacher, "that you believe my word. The watch is yours. Take good care of it. Wind it up every night."

The rest of the class looked on in amazement; and one of them said: "Teacher, you don't mean that the watch is his? You don't mean that he hasn't to give it back to you?"

"No," said the teacher, "he hasn't to give it back to me. It is his own now."

"Oh—h—h! if I had only known that, wouldn't I have taken it!"

Your Walk Tells

"That man must have been in the army, or in a military school," I said to a friend once.

"Yes," he said; "how did you know?"

"By the way he walks."

You can tell that some people have been with Jesus by their walk.

Living on Crumbs

I once heard Rev. William Arnot say that he was the guest of a friend who had a favorite dog. The animal would come into the room where the family were sitting at the dinner table, and would stand looking at his master. If the master threw him a crumb, the dog would seize it before it got to the floor. But if he put the joint of meat down on the floor the dog would look at it and leave it alone, as if it were too good for him.

"So," said Mr. Arnot, "there are many Christians who are satisfied to live on crumbs, when God wants to give them the whole joint."

Come boldly to the throne of grace, and get the help you need. There is an abundance for all.

An Incident of the Civil War

After the battle of Murfreesboro, in the Civil War, I was stationed in the hospital. For two nights I had been unable to get any rest, and being really worn out, on the third night I had lain down to sleep. About midnight I was called to see a wounded soldier who was very low. At first I tried to put the messenger off, but he told me that if I waited it might be too late in the morning. I went to the ward where I had been directed, and found the man who had sent for me. I shall never forget his face as I saw it that night in the dim, uncertain candle-light. I asked what I could do for him, and he said that he wanted me to "help him die." I told him I would bear him in my arms into the Kingdom of God if I could, but I couldn't, and then I tried to preach the Gospel. He only shook his head and said:

"He can't save me; I have sinned all my life."

My thoughts went back to his loved ones in the North, and I thought that even then his mother might be praying for her boy. I repeated promise after promise, and prayed with the dying man, but nothing I said seemed to help him. Then I said that I wanted to read to him an account of an interview which Christ had one night while here on earth with a man who was anxious about his eternal welfare, and I read the 3d chapter of John, how Nicodemus came to the Master. As I read on, his eyes became riveted upon me, and he seemed to drink in every syllable. When I came to the words: "As Moses lifted up the serpent in the wilderness, even so must the Son of Man be lifted up: that whosoever believeth in Him should not perish, but have eternal life," he stopped me and asked:

"Is that there?"

"Yes," I said.

"Well," he said, "I never knew that was in the Bible. Read it again."

Leaning his elbows on the side of the cot he brought his hands together in a firm grasp, and when I finished he exclaimed:

"That's good. Won't you read it again?"

Slowly I repeated the passage the third time. When

I finished I saw that his eyes were closed, and the troubled expression on his face had given way to a peaceful smile. His lips moved, and I bent over him to catch what he was saying, and heard in a faint whisper:

"'As Moses lifted up the serpent in the wilderness, even so must the Son of Man be lifted up; that whosoever believeth in Him should not perish, but have eternal life.'"

He opened his eyes and said: "That's enough; don't read any more."

Early next morning I again came to his cot, but it was empty. The attendant in charge told me the young man had died peacefully, and said that after my visit he had rested quietly, repeating to himself, now and then, that glorious proclamation: "Whosoever believeth in Him should not perish, but have eternal life."

It Took Two

A Scotchman was once asked how many it took to convert him.

"Two," he replied.

"Two! How was that? didn't God do it all?"

"The Almighty and myself converted me," he said. "I did all I could against it, and the Almighty did all He could for it, and He was victorious."

Getting Too Personal

My wife was once teaching my little boy a Sabbath school lesson; she was telling him to notice how sin grows till it becomes a habit. The little fellow thought it was coming too close to him, so he colored up, and finally said·

"Mamma, I think you are getting a good way from the subject."

Both Afraid

I remember a man in New York who used to come and pray with me. He had his cross. He was afraid to confess Christ. It seemed that down at the bottom of his trunk he had a Bible. He wanted to get it out and read it to a companion with whom he lived, but he was ashamed to do it. For a whole week that was his cross; and after he had carried the burden that long, and after a terrible struggle, he made up his mind. He said, "I will take my Bible out to-night and read it." He took it out, and soon he heard the footsteps of his mate coming upstairs.

His first impulse was to put it away again, but then he thought he would not—he would face his companion with it. His mate came in, and seeing him at his Bible, said:

"John, are you interested in these things?"

"Yes," he replied.

"How long has this been, then?" asked his companion.

"Exactly a week," he answered; "for a whole week I have tried to get out my Bible to read to you, but I have never done so till now."

"Well," said his friend, "it is a strange thing. *I was converted on the same night*, and I, too, was ashamed to take my Bible out."

Awakened Recollections

Several years ago, a minister in a town much resorted to by invalids was requested to see a gentleman reported to be very ill. He went accordingly. The patient was a man between fifty and sixty, and had been a successful merchant in the metropolis. He had been ordered to this health resort, but, as it proved, only to die there. The minister soon saw that it was no earnest desire for spiritual benefit that had prompted the request. On the contrary, he felt there was little or no sense of the gravity of the case, and no sympathy with his own concern for the sufferer. He felt as if, on the part of the relatives at least, there was almost suppressed ridicule of his efforts to guide the dying man to the truth.

Altogether the case was about as hopeless a one as my friend had ever dealt with. Still he persevered. I cannot remember whether it was during the first visit, or upon a second call, that it occurred to him, seeing the sufferer was a Scotchman, to take advantage of a line in the metrical version of the psalms used in Scotland, to convey the saving truth he was trying to state.

"There is a line in one of your Scotch psalms," said my friend, "that contains in five words all I would tell you. I do not know the psalm, or the rest of the verse; but here are the words, and the whole gospel is in them:

"None perish that Him trust."

The invalid looked up from his pillow, and slowly repeated:

"Ill shall the wicked slay: laid waste
Shall be who hate the just;
The Lord redeems His servants' souls:
None perish that Him trust."

"That is it," said my friend; "believe on the Lord Jesus Christ. None perish that *Him* trust. Where did you learn that psalm?"

"My mother taught me it when I was a boy. She used to go to Dr. Alexander's church at Edinburgh."

Old recollections seemed awakened. Attentively he

listened to what more it was thought proper to add. He requested a repetition of the visit. How often after the minister saw him I do not recollect, but from that hour there was a marked change, and an evident growing interest as the way of salvation was explained.

The last time my friend was sent for, he went without delay, but it was too late, or seemed to be too late, for the dying man to receive aught from human lips. He was already far down the valley, alone, and friends could only look after him as he descended. As they gazed in silence, they saw his lips moving. My friend bent down to catch the faint whispers that followed each other in slow succession; they were:

"None—perish—that—Him—trust."

He heard no more; but left, indulging a cheerful confidence that the seed cast into the heart of her boy by a mother long, long years before, had borne fruit to eternal life.

Thank God for the Resurrection!

At the battle of Inkerman a soldier was just able to crawl to his tent after he was struck down. When found, he was lying upon his face, his open Bible before him, his hand glued fast to the page by his life-blood which covered it. Then his hand was lifted, the letters of the printed page were clearly traced upon it, and with the ever-living promise in and on his hand, they laid him in a soldier's grave. The words were:

"I am the resurrection and the life; he that believeth in Me, though he were dead, yet shall he live."

I want a religion that can comfort even in death, that can unite me with my loved ones. Oh, what gloom and darkness would settle upon this world if it was not for the glorious doctrine of the resurrection! Thank God, the glorious morning will soon break. For a little while God asks us to be on the watch-tower, faithful to Him and waiting for the summons. Soon our Lord will come to receive His own, whether they be living or dead.

Too Generous

A colored preacher once said that a good many of his congregation would be lost because they were too generous. He saw that the people looked rather surprised; so he said:

"Perhaps you think I have made a mistake, and that I ought to have said you will be lost because you are not generous enough. That is not so; I meant just what I said. You give away too many sermons. You hear them, as it were, for other people."

There are a good many who listen for those behind them; they say the message is very good for neighbor So-and-so; and they pass it over their shoulders, till it gets clear out of the door.

We All Need Christ

I read of a minister traveling in the South who obtained permission to preach in the local jail. A son of his host went with him. On the way back the young man, who was not a Christian, said to the minister:

"I hope some of the convicts were impressed. Such a sermon as that ought to do them good."

"Did it do you good?" the minister asked.

"Oh, you were preaching to the convicts!" the young man answered.

The minister shook his head, and said: "I preached Christ, and you need Him as much as they."

Keep Your Light Shining

I remember hearing of two men who had charge of a revolving light in a lighthouse on a storm-bound and rocky coast. Somehow the machinery went wrong, and the light did not revolve. They were so afraid that those at sea should mistake it for some other light, that they worked all the night through to keep the light moving round.

Let us keep our lights in the proper place, so that the world may see that the religion of Christ is not a sham but a reality.

They Did Not Believe Him

A man was converted in Europe several years ago, and he liked the Gospel so well he thought he should go and preach it. He started out, and great crowds came to hear him just out of curiosity. The next night there were not so many there, and the third night the man had scarcely a hearer. But he was anxious to preach the Gospel, and so he prepared some great placards and posted them all over the town, declaring that if any man in that town that was in debt would come to his office before twelve o'clock on a certain day with the proof of indebtedness, he would pay the debt. This news spread all over the town, but the people did not believe him.

One man said to his neighbor, "John, do you believe this man will pay our debts?"

"No, of course not, it's only a hoax."

The day came, and instead of there being a great rush, nobody came. Now it is a wonder there is not a great rush of men into the Kingdom of God to have their debts paid, when a man can be saved for nothing.

About ten o'clock a man was walking in front of the office. He looked this way and that to see if anybody was looking, and by and by, satisfied that there was no one looking, he slipped in, and said:

"I saw a notice about town that if any one would call here at a certain hour you would pay their debts; is there any truth in it?"

"Yes," said the man; "it's quite true. Did you bring the necessary papers with you?"

"Yes."

After the man had paid the debt, he said, "Sit down, I want to talk with you," and he kept him there until twelve o'clock. Before twelve o'clock had passed two more came in and had their debts paid. At twelve o'clock he let them all out. Some other men were standing around the door.

"Well, did he pay your debts?"

"Yes," they said; "it was quite true; our debts were all paid."

"Oh! then we'll go in and get ours paid."

They went, but it was too late. Twelve o'clock had passed. To every one of you who is a bankrupt sinner—and you never saw a sinner in the world that was not a bankrupt sinner—Christ comes and He says: "I will pay your debts."

"Water! Water!"

After one of the great battles in the war we were coming down the Tennessee River with a company of wounded men. It was in the spring of the year, and the water was not clear. You know that the cry of a wounded man is: "Water! water!" especially in a hot country. I remember taking a glass of the muddy water to one of these men. Although he was very thirsty, he only drank a little of it. He handed the glass back to me, and as he did so, he said:

"Oh, for a draught of water from my father's well!"

Are there any thirsty ones here? Come and drink of the fountain opened in Christ! Your longing will be satisfied, and you will never thirst again.

Scissors or Oranges?

My wife told me one day that she had just come from a friend's house where one of the children, a little boy, had been cutting something with a knife, and it had slipped upward and put out his eye, and his mother was afraid of his losing the other. Of course, after that my wife was careful that our little boy, two years old, shouldn't get the scissors, or anything by which he could harm himself. But prohibit a child from having any particular thing, and he's sure to have it; so one day our little fellow got hold of the scissors. His sister seeing what he had, and knowing the law, tried to take the scissors from him, but the more she tried the more he clung to them. All at once she remembered that he liked oranges, and that there was one in the next room. Away she went and back she came:

"Willie, would you like an orange?"

The scissors were dropped, and he clutched the orange.

God sometimes takes away the scissors, but He gives us an orange. Get both your feet into the narrow way; it leads to life and joy; its ways are ways of pleasantness, and all its paths are peace. It is the way of victory, of peace; no gloom there; all light.

He Honored the Emperor

Is is said that Alexander the Great had a favorite general to whom he had given permission to draw upon the royal treasury for any amount. On one occasion this general had made a draft for such an enormous sum that the treasurer refused to honor it until he consulted the emperor. So he went into his presence and told him what the general had done.

"Did you not honor the draft?" said the emperor.

"No; I refused until I had seen your majesty, because the amount was so great."

The emperor was indignant. His treasurer said that he was afraid of offending him if he had paid the amount.

"Do you not know," replied the emperor, "that he honors me and my kingdom by making a large draft?"

Whether the story be authentic or not, it is true that we honor God when we ask for great things.

Faith in the Wrong Person

How often we hear a man say: "There is a member of the church who cheated me out of five dollars, and I am not going to have anything more to do with people who call themselves Christians." But if the man had had faith in Jesus Christ you do not suppose he would have had his faith shattered because some one cheated him out of five dollars, do you? What we want is to have faith in the Lord Jesus Christ. If a man has that, he has something he can anchor to, and the anchor will hold; and when the hour of temptation comes to him, and the hour of trial, the man will stand firm. If we are only converted to man, and our faith is in man, we will certainly be disappointed.

"Trusting in the Dark"

Suppose I have a sick boy. I know nothing about medicine; but I call in the doctor, and put that boy's life and everything into his hands. I do not fail to believe in him; and I do not interfere at all. Do you call that trusting in the dark? Not at all! I used my best judgment, and I put that boy's life into the hands of a good physician.

You have a soul diseased. Put it into the hand of the Great Physician! Trust Him, and He will take care of it. He has had some of the most hopeless cases. He was able to heal all that came to Him while on earth. He is the same to-day.

Take another illustration. Suppose you have one thousand dollars, and there are forty thieves who want to rob you of it. I tell you that there is a bank here, and that I will introduce you to the president so that you can deposit the money. You do not know anything of the bank, save by repute; you know nothing about how the books are kept; but you take my word, and you believe my testimony, that if you deposit the money it will be safe; and you go in and place the thousand dollars there.

We must trust God in time of trouble, in time of bereavement. You can trust Him with your soul until your dying day, if you will. Will you not do it?

Don't Trust this Plank

Don't be watching your feelings. There is not one verse from Genesis to Revelation about being saved by feeling. When the devil sees a poor soul in agony in the waves of sin, and getting close to the Rock of Ages, he just holds out the plank of "feeling" to him, and says,

"There, get on that; you feel more comfortable now, don't you?" And, while the man stands getting his breath again, out goes the plank from under him, and he is worse off than ever. Accept no refuge but the Rock, —the Everlasting Strength.

Enthusiasm

As I was leaving New York to go to England in 1867, a friend said to me: "I hope you will go to Edinburgh and be at the General Assembly this year. When I was there a year ago I heard such a speech as I shall never forget. Doctor Duff made a speech that set me all on fire. I shall never forget the hour I spent in that meeting."

Doctor Duff had been out in India as a missionary; he had spent twenty-five years there preaching the Gospel and establishing schools. He came back with a broken-down constitution. He was permitted to address the General Assembly, in order to make an appeal for men to go into the mission field. After he had spoken for a considerable time, he became exhausted and fainted away. They carried him out of the hall into another room. The doctors worked over him for some time, and at last he began to recover. When he realized where he was, he roused himself and said:

"I did not finish my speech; carry me back and let me finish it."

They told him he could only do it at the peril of his life. Said he:

"I will do it if I die."

So they took him back to the hall. My friend said it was one of the most solemn scenes he ever witnessed in his life. They brought the white-haired man into the

Assembly Hall, and as he appeared at the door every person sprang to his feet; the tears flowed freely as they looked upon the grand old veteran. With a trembling voice, he said:

"Fathers and mothers of Scotland, is it true that you have no more sons to send to India to work for the Lord Jesus Christ? The call for help is growing louder and louder, but there are few coming forward to answer it. You have the money put away in the bank, but where are the laborers who shall go into the field? When Queen Victoria wants men to volunteer for her army in India, you freely give your sons. You do not talk about their losing their health, and about the trying climate. But when the Lord Jesus is calling for laborers, Scotland is saying: 'We have no more sons to give.'"

Turning to the President of the Assembly, he said:

"Mr. Moderator, if it is true that Scotland has no more sons to give to the service of the Lord Jesus Christ in India, although I have lost my health in that land and came home to die, if there are none who will go and tell those heathen of Christ, then I will be off to-morrow, to let them know that there is one old Scotchman who is ready to die for them. I will go back to the shores of the Ganges, and there lay down my life as a witness for the Son of God."

Thank God for such a man as that! We want men to-day who are willing, if need be, to lay down their lives for the Son of God. Then we shall be able to make an impression upon the world. When they see that we are in earnest, their hearts will be touched, and we shall be able to lead them to the Lord Jesus Christ.

Only the Sick Ones Would Follow

A friend, who was traveling in the East, heard that there was a shepherd who still kept up the custom of calling his sheep by name. He went to the man, and said:

"Let me put on your clothes, and take your crook, and I will call them, and see if they will come to me."

And so he did, and he called one sheep, "Mina, Mina," but the whole flock ran away from him. Then he said to the shepherd:

"Will none of them follow me when I call them?"

The shepherd replied: "Yes, sir, some of them will; the sick sheep will follow anybody."

I'm not going to make the application, I leave that to you.

Paul's Persuasion

A man was dying during the war. He was asked of what persuasion he was. He replied:

"Paul's."

"What! are you a Methodist? They all claim Paul."

"No."

"Are you a Presbyterian then? They claim Paul, too."

"No."

"Of what persuasion are you then?"

"I am persuaded that He is able to keep that which I have committed unto Him against that day."

How to Warm up the Church

I was once preaching in Scotland, and when I got to the church it was so cold that I could see my breath three feet away. I said to the "beadle," as they call him:

"Aren't you going to have any heat in this building?"

He said they had no stoves or any other provision for heat.

"Well, how do you expect people to get warm?"

"Oh!" he said, "we expect the pulpit to warm us up."

It Seemed a Small Thing

I remember hearing of a man at sea who was very sea-sick. If there is a time when a man feels that he cannot do any work for the Lord it is then—in my opinion. While this man was sick he heard that a man had fallen overboard. He was wondering if he could do anything to help to save him. He laid hold of a light, and held it up to the port-hole.

The drowning man was saved. When this man got over his attack of sickness he was up on deck one day, and was talking to the man who was rescued. The saved man gave this testimony. He said he had gone down the second time, and was just going down again for the last time, when he put out his hand. Just then, he said, some one held a light at the port-hole, and the light fell on his hand. A man caught him by the hand and pulled him into the lifeboat.

It seemed a small thing to do to hold up the light; yet it saved the man's life. If you cannot do some great thing you can hold the light for some poor, perishing drunkard, who may be won to Christ and delivered from destruction. Let us take the torch of salvation and go into these dark homes, and hold up Christ to the people as the Savior of the world.

The Jealous Eagle

There is a fable of an eagle which could outfly another, and the other didn't like it. The latter saw a sportsman one day, and said to him·

"I wish you would bring down that eagle."

The sportsman replied that he would if he only had some feathers to put into the arrow. So the eagle pulled one out of his wing. The arrow was shot, but didn't quite reach the rival eagle; it was flying too high. The envious eagle pulled out more feathers, and kept pulling them out until he lost so many that he couldn't fly, and then the sportsman turned around and killed him.

My friend, if you are jealous, the only man you can hurt is yourself.

Faith

When I was a boy, in the spring of the year, when the snow had melted away on the New England hills where I lived, I used to take a certain kind of glass and hold it up to the warm rays of the sun. These would strike on it, and I would set the woods on fire.

Faith is the glass that brings the fire of God out of heaven. It was faith that drew the fire down on Carmel and burned up Elijah's offering. We have the same God to-day, and the same faith. Some people seem to think that faith is getting old, and that the Bible is wearing out. But the Lord will revive His work now; and we shall be able to set the world on fire if each believer has a strong and simple faith.

Reuben Johnson's Pardon

When I was in Ohio a few years ago, I was invited to preach in the State prison. Eleven hundred convicts were brought into the chapel, and all sat in front of me. After I had got through the preaching, the chaplain said to me:

"Mr. Moody, I want to tell you of a scene which occurred in this room. A few years ago, our commissioners went to the Governor of the State, and got him to promise that he would pardon five men for good behavior. The Governor consented, with this understanding—that the record was to be kept secret, and that at the end of six months the five men highest on the roll should receive a pardon, regardless of who or what they were. At the end of six months the prisoners were all brought into the chapel. The commissioners came; the president stood on the platform, and putting his hand in his pocket, brought out some papers, and said:

" 'I hold in my hand pardons for five men.' "

The chaplain told me he never witnessed anything on earth like it. Every man was as still as death. Many were deadly pale. The suspense was awful; it seemed as if every heart had ceased to beat. The commissioner went on to tell them how they had got the pardon; but the chaplain interrupted him.

"Before you make your speech, read out the names. This suspense is awful."

So he read out the first name, "Reuben Johnson will come and get his pardon"; and he held it out, but none came forward.

He said to the warden: "Are all the prisoners here?"

The warden told him they were all there.

Then he said again, "Reuben Johnson will come and get his pardon. It is signed and sealed by the Governor. He is a free man."

Not one moved. The chaplain looked right down where Reuben was. He was well known; he had been nineteen years there, and many were looking around to see him spring to his feet. But he himself was looking around to see the fortunate man who had got his pardon. Finally the chaplain had caught his eye, and said:

"Reuben, you are the man."

Reuben turned around and looked behind him to see where Reuben was. The chaplain said the second time, "Reuben, *you* are the man"; and the second time he looked around, thinking it must be some other Reuben. He had to say three times, "Reuben, come and get your pardon."

At last the truth began to steal over the old man. He got up, came along down the hall, trembling from head to foot, and when he got the pardon he looked at it, and went back to his seat, buried his face in his hands, and wept. When the prisoners got into the ranks to go back to the cells, Reuben got into the ranks, too, and the chaplain had to call him:

"Reuben, get out of the ranks; you are a free man, you are no longer a prisoner."

And Reuben stepped out of the ranks. He was free!

That is the way men make out pardons; they make them out for good character or good behavior; but God makes out pardons for men who have not got any character. He offers a pardon to every sinner on earth if he will take it. I do not care who he is or what he is like. He may be the greatest libertine that ever walked the streets, or the greatest blackguard who ever lived, or the greatest drunkard, or thief, or vagabond. Christ commissioned His disciples to preach the Gospel to *every creature*.

Clogged by Sand

A number of years ago the mouth of the Mississippi River became so clogged that no vessels could pass through the channel. Much anxiety was felt, for the farmers along its banks depended upon the river for the transportation of their products.

There were no great, overhanging rocks to fall into the stream and block the way of the vessels. No volcanic upheaval had changed its bed. The trouble was simply the deposit of sediment—washings from the muddy banks and bottom of the river, so fine that a filter would hardly free the water from its impurity. And yet these tiny specks, massed together, hindered the great river's flow to the ocean; for a time threatened the industries of the Southwestern States.

It does not need some great sin to block the channel of blessing. Small sins will block the stream.

Human ingenuity at last found a way to keep the Mississippi channel open, but only Divine power can free our hearts from sin.

The Difference

A man said to me some time ago, "How do you account for the fact that Mohammed began his work six hundred years after Christ and yet he has now more disciples than Christ?"

I replied, "A man can be a disciple of Mohammed and not deny himself, not have any cross. He can live in the darkest, blackest, foulest sin; but if any man will be a disciple of Jesus Christ he must come out from the world, he must take up his cross daily and follow Jesus."

Spurgeon's Parable

Mr. Spurgeon once made a parable. He said: "There was once a tyrant who summoned one of his subjects into his presence, and ordered him to make a chain. The poor blacksmith—that was his occupation—had to go to work and forge the chain. When it was done, he brought it into the presence of the tyrant, and was ordered to take it away and make it twice the length.

He brought it again to the tyrant, and again he was ordered to double it. Back he came when he had obeyed the order, and the tyrant looked at it, and then commanded the servants to bind the man hand and foot with the chain he had made and cast him into prison.

"That is what the devil does with men," Mr. Spurgeon said. "He makes them forge their own chain, and then binds them hand and foot with it, and casts them into outer darkness."

My friends, that is just what drunkards, gamblers, blasphemers—that is just what every sinner is doing. But thank God, we can tell them of a deliverer. The Son of God has power to break every one of their fetters if they will only come to Him.

Those Five Bottles of Wine

A lady in the north of England said that every time she got down before God to pray, five bottles of wine came up before her mind. She had taken them wrongfully one time when she was a housekeeper, and had not been able to pray since. She was advised to make restitution.

"But the person is dead," she said.

"Are not some of the heirs living?"

"Yes, a son."

"Then go to that son and pay him back."

"Well," she said, "I want to see the face of God, but I could not think of doing a thing like that. My reputation is at stake."

She went away, and came back the next day to ask if it would not do just as well to put that money in the treasury of the Lord.

"No," she was told, "God doesn't want any stolen money. The only thing is to make restitution."

She carried that burden for several days, but finally went into the country, saw that son, made a full confession and offered him a five-pound note. He said he didn't want the money, but she finally persuaded him to take it, and came back with a joy and peace that made her face radiant. She became a magnificent worker for souls, and led many into the light.

My dear friends, get these stumbling stones out of the way. God does not want a man to shout "Hallelujah" who doesn't pay his debts. Many of our prayer-meetings are killed by men trying to pray who cannot pray because their lives are not right. Sin builds up a great wall between us and God. A man may stand high in the community and may be a member of some church "in good standing," but the question is, how does he stand in the sight of God? If there is anything wrong in your life, make it right.

Covering a Sun-Dial

Phillips Brooks told a story of some savages to whom was given a sun-dial. So desirous were they to honor and keep it sacred that they housed it in and built a roof over it.

"Is your belief in God so reverent that you put it to one side carefully as being too sacred for daily use? Learn to use it. Let God in on your life. Let your faith inspire you to good works."

David Livingstone's Loving Spirit

In the late Professor Drummond's "The Greatest Thing in the World," he tells of meeting with natives in the interior of Africa who remembered David Livingstone. They could not understand a word he uttered, but they recognized the universal language of love through which he appealed to them. It had been many years since that Christian hero had passed their way, but the very remembrance of his presence among them would kindle a friendly smile.

It is this very selfsame universal language of love, divine, Christlike love, that we must have if we are going to be used of God. The world does not understand theology or dogma, but it understands love and sympathy. A loving act may be more powerful and far-reaching than the most eloquent sermon.

When a Christian Grows

Doctor Bonar once remarked that he could tell when a Christian was growing. In proportion to his growth in grace he would elevate his Master, talk less of what he was doing, and become smaller and smaller in his own esteem, until, like the morning star, he faded away before the rising sun. Jonathan was willing to decrease that David might increase; and John the Baptist showed the same spirit of humility.

"It's Better Higher Up!"

Not long ago there lived an old bed-ridden saint, and a Christian lady who visited her found her always very cheerful. This visitor had a lady friend of wealth, who constantly looked on the dark side of things, and was always cast down, although she was a professed Christian. She thought it would do this lady good to see the bed-ridden saint, so she took her down to the house. She lived up in the garret, five stories up, and when they had got to the first story the lady drew up her dress, and said:

"How dark and filthy it is!"

"It's better higher up," said her friend.

They got to the next story, and it was no better; the lady complained again, but her friend replied:

"It's better higher up."

At the third floor it seemed still worse, and the lady kept complaining, but her friend kept saying:

"It's better higher up."

At last they got to the fifth story, and when they went into the sick-room, there was a nice carpet on the floor, flowering plants in the window, and little birds singing. And there they found this bed-ridden saint— one of those saints whom God is polishing for His own temple—just beaming with joy.

The lady said to her, "It must be very hard for you to lie here."

She smiled, and said, "*It's better higher up.*"

Yes! And if things go against us, my friends, let us remember that "it's better higher up."

She Wanted Him to be Graceful

A Christian mother said she wanted her son to go to a dancing-school because he was so awkward; she wanted him to be more graceful. Wanted him to get grace in his *heels*, you see, instead of his *heart*. After six weeks he had made such poor progress she took him out in disgust and chided him. Said he:

"I'm sorry, mother, I'm so stupid about it, but I can't seem to do any better. You see, it's one of the things I can't pray over."

A Most Extraordinary Well!

I heard of a well that was said to be very good, except that it had two faults; it *would* freeze up in the winter, and it *would* dry up in the summer. A most extraordinary well, but I am afraid there are many wells like it! There are many people who are good at certain times ; as some one has expressed it, they seem to be good "in spots." What we want is to be red hot all the time. People talk about striking while the iron is hot. Cromwell said that he would rather strike the iron and make it hot.

Two Ways of Being United

There are two ways of being united—one is by being frozen together, and the other is by being melted together. What Christians need is to be united in brotherly love, and then they may expect to have power.

Looking Downward

I heard once of a man who dreamed that he was swept into heaven, and oh, he was so delighted to think that he had at last got there. All at once one came and said:

"Come, I want to show you something."

He took him to the battlements, and he said, "Look down yonder; what do you see?"

"I see a very dark world."

"Look and see if you know it."

"Why, yes," he said, "that is the world I have come from."

"What do you see?"

"Men are blindfolded there; many of them are going over a precipice."

"Well, will you stay here and enjoy heaven, or will you go back to earth and spend a little longer time, and tell those men about this world?"

He was a Christian worker who had been discouraged. He awoke from his sleep and later he said:

"I have never wished myself dead since."

A Well-Deserved Rebuff

When I first held meetings in Glasgow, my committee (without my knowledge) sent to a livery establishment that kept a thousand horses, to engage a cab to drive me to my meetings on Sunday. The proprietor was a godly man, and sent me this message:

"Tell Mr. Moody he will do as much good by walking to his meetings as by driving three or four miles through the Fourth Commandment."

Whichever Way the Wind Blows

Spurgeon went down into the country to visit a friend who had built a new barn, and on the barn was a cupola upon which they had put a weather vane with this text of Scripture on it: "God is love." Spurgeon said to the man:

"What do you mean by putting that text of Scripture on the weather vane? Do you mean that God's love is as changeable as the wind?"

"Oh, no," was the reply; "I mean to say that God is love *whichever way the wind blows.*"

Different Ideas about Prayer

There is a new kind of philosophy nowadays which teaches that it is a very healthy exercise to pray, because it teaches us submission. God doesn't change in His plans for us; we won't get anything more by asking, but then just ask, it is healthy exercise! A mother in New York has lost track of her boy. She is wandering around the streets seeking for him. You know that the boy is dead, but still you tell her to keep on seeking—it is healthy exercise. What downright mockery it is for any one to talk such stuff as that!

Suppose that in the dead of winter, when the thermometer is down at zero, a man who has been stuck for twenty-four hours in a drift manages to get to my house at midnight, and rings the bell. I go to the window, and say:

"Who is there?"

"Mr. ——. I have been in a snowbank twenty-four hours, and I am dying. Won't you help him?"

"Well," I say, "I have a fixed rule never to open my door until morning, but you just keep on knocking; it will do you good; it is a healthy exercise."

That is a fair illustration of the way some people would have us look at prayer. Christ said, "Ask, and ye *shall* receive."

During the war a man came to me at Nashville, a great, big six-footer, and he was shaking all over and crying like a baby. I thought he must have delirium tremens. He pulled out an old, soiled letter and said:

"Chaplain, read that, will you?"

It was a letter from his sister, saying that every night as the sun went down she fell on her knees and prayed God to save her brother. The soldier said:

"Chaplain, I have been in a number of battles, and have been before the cannon's mouth without trembling a bit; but the moment I read that letter I began to shake. I suppose that I am the meanest wretch in the whole Cumberland Army."

I took a copy of the letter and went to another division of the army, thirty miles away. The next day I got up before the men and read it, and told how that man had been saved in answer to the prayers of his sister six hundred miles away. When I closed, a fine-looking man got up and said:

"That letter reminds me of the last letter I got from my mother. She said, 'My boy, when you get this letter, won't you go off behind a tree and pray to your mother's God that you may be converted? Now, my son, won't you become a Christian?'"

He said he put the letter in his pocket, and expected to pay no more attention to it, as he thought he would get a good many more letters from her; but a few days later a dispatch came saying that his mother was dead. Then he took her advice, and went off behind a tree and cried to his mother's God; the prayer was answered, and he said:

"This is the first time I have ever confessed Jesus Christ."

There were two men, one who had a sister pleading six hundred miles away, and the other whose mother had brought him on his knees and into the Kingdom of God. My dear friends, never stop praying; do not be discouraged. God wants you to "pray without ceasing."

Moving over to Thanksgiving Street

An old gentleman got up once in a meeting and said he had lived nearly all his life on Grumble street, but not long ago he had moved over on Thanksgiving street. His face showed it. Paul and Silas in jail at Philippi, when they had received stripes on the back and had their feet in the stocks, still sang praises to God. If some of us were in jail, with our feet in the stocks, I don't think we would sing much. We want a cheerful Christianity.

An Awful Awakening

In a town of Switzerland a few years ago, some workingmen going early to work, walking along the street, saw a white figure on the top of a high house. What was it? A lady in her night-dress; and she was sitting looking down, quite happy, smiling in perfect security. She was a somnambulist. She had risen in her sleep without anyone in the house knowing it, and had taken her station, and was pleasantly looking about, and no doubt dreaming—dreaming pleasant dreams.

They didn't know what they could do to save her from her peril. Just as they were talking together, the sun rose. A bright beam fell upon her eyes. She waked and saw where she was; gazed one moment around, and then fell headlong—killed on the spot. It was an awful awakening!

Fellow-sinner, if you are out of Christ, and the day of His coming overtakes you—oh, what if the first beam of that bright day be the first moment of your awakening, and it is too late!

Don't Trifle with God

I met a man some time ago who told me he had never sinned in his life. He was the first perfect man I had ever met. I thought I would question him, and began to measure him by the Law. I asked him:

"Do you ever get angry?"

"Well," he said, "sometimes I do; but I have a right to do so. It is righteous indignation."

"Do you swear when you get angry?"

He admitted he did sometimes.

"Then," I asked, "are you ready to meet God?"

"Yes," he replied, "because I never mean anything when I swear."

Suppose I steal a man's watch and he comes after me. "Yes," I say, "I stole your watch and pawned it, but *I did not mean anything by it.* I pawned it and spent the money, but *I did not mean anything by it.*"

You would smile at and deride such a statement.

Ah, friends! You cannot trifle with God in that way.

First Obey

Suppose I say to my boy, "Willie, I want you to go out and bring me a glass of water."

He says he doesn't want to go.

"I didn't ask you whether you wanted to go or not, Willie, I told you to go."

"But I don't want to go," he says.

"I tell you, you must go and get me a glass of water."

He does not like to go. But he knows I am very fond of grapes, and he is very fond of them himself, so he goes out, and some one gives him a beautiful cluster of grapes. He comes in and says:

"Here, papa, here is a beautiful cluster of grapes for you."

"But what about the water?"

"Won't the grapes be acceptable, papa?"

"No, my boy, the grapes are not acceptable; I won't take them; I want you to get me a glass of water."

The little fellow doesn't want to get the water, but he goes out, and this time some one gives him an orange. He brings it in and places it before me.

"Is that acceptable?" he asks.

"No, no, no!" I say; "I want nothing but water;

you cannot do anything to please me until you get the water."

And so, my friends, to please God you must first obey Him.

A Fragrant Act

There is a preacher in Edinburgh, but I never think of him as a preacher, although he is one of the finest preachers in Scotland. There is just one act associated with that man that I will carry in remembrance to the grave.

There is a hospital for little children in Edinburgh, and that great minister, with a large parish and a large congregation, goes one afternoon every week and sits down and talks with those little children—a good many of them there for life; they are incurable. One day he found a little boy, only six years old, who had been brought over from Fife. The little fellow was in great distress because the doctors were coming to take off his leg. Think how you would feel, if you had a little brother six years old and he was taken off to the hospital, and the doctor said that he was coming forty-eight hours afterward to take off his leg!

Well, that minister tried to comfort the boy, and said: "Your father will come to be with you."

"No," he said, "my father is dead; he cannot be here."

"Well, your mother will come."

"My mother is over in Fife. She is sick and cannot come."

The minister himself could not come, so he said, "Well, you know the matron here is a mother; she has got a great big heart."

The little chin began to quiver as the boy said: "Perhaps Jesus will be with me."

Do you have any doubt of it? Next Friday the man of God went to the hospital, but he found the cot was empty. The poor boy was gone; the Savior had come and taken him to His bosom.

One little act of kindness will often live a good deal longer than a most magnificent sermon.

We Shall Know Them

I heard a child whose mother died so early that she could not remember the mother. She did not have a photograph, and never saw her face; but after she had come to years of understanding, she was taken sick, and when she was dying, suddenly her face lit up. She seemed to see her mother, and said:

"Oh mother!"

I think that when I see my Master I shall know Him. I have an idea that when I see Moses and the Prophets and the Patriarchs and Apostles, I shall know them. Do you ask, How? I don't know.

Encourage Others

If we cannot be in the battle ourselves let us not seek to discourage others.

A Highland chief of the Macgregor clan fell wounded at the battle of Sheriff-Muir. Seeing their leader fall, the clan wavered, and gave the foe an advantage. The old chieftain, perceiving this, raised himself on his elbow, while the blood streamed from his wounds, and cried out:

"I am not dead, my children; I am looking at you to see you do your duty."

This roused them to new energy and almost superhuman effort.

So, when our strength fails and our hearts sink within us, the Captain of our salvation cries:

"Lo, I am with you alway, even to the end of the world. I will never leave nor forsake thee."

Their Prayers Answered

I remember when preaching on one occasion to an immense audience in the Agricultural Hall in London, a father and mother were in great distress about their absent son, who had given up God's ways and had wandered from his father's home to the wild bush of Australia. These poor parents asked the united prayers of that vast congregation for their son, and I suppose fully 20,000 rose to the mercy seat. It was ascertained afterward that at the very hour those prayers ascended from the audience in London, that young man was riding through the Australian bush to a town a day's ride from his camp. Something caused him to think of his home and his parents, and as he sat in the saddle, the Spirit of God descended upon him, and he was convicted of sin. Dismounting, he knelt down by his horse's side, and prayed to God for forgiveness, and in a little while he was assured of conversion. When he reached the town, he wrote the good news to his delighted mother, and asked if they would receive him at home. The answer flashed along the cable beneath the ocean:

"Come home at once."

So afraid were they that he might arrive in the night when they were not awake to receive him, that they fastened a big bell to the door, so that all the family would be awakened as he entered.

"He is My Brother!"

A fearful storm was raging, when the cry was heard: "Man overboard!"

A human form was seen manfully breasting the furious elements in the direction of the shore; but the raging waves bore the struggler rapidly outward, and ere the boats could be lowered, a fearful space separated the victim from help. Above the shriek of the storm and roar of the waters rose his rending cry. It was an agonizing moment. With bated breath and blanched cheek, every eye was strained to the struggling man. Manfully did the brave rowers strain every nerve in that race of mercy; but all their efforts were in vain. One wild shriek of despair, and the victim went down. A piercing cry, "Save him, save him!" rang through the hushed crowd; and into their midst darted an agitated man, throwing his arms wildly in the air, shouting, "A thousand pounds for the man who saves his life!" but his staring eyes rested only on the spot where the waves rolled remorselessly over the perished. He whose strong cry broke the stillness of the crowd was Captain of the ship from whence the drowned man fell, and was *his brother*.

This is the feeling we should have in the various ranks of those bearing commission under the great Captain of our salvation. "Save him! he is my brother."

The fact is, men do not believe in Christianity because they think we are not in earnest about it. When the people see that we are in earnest in all that we undertake for God, they will begin to tremble; men and women will be inquiring the way to Zion.

He Trusted his Father

I was standing with a friend at his garden gate one evening when two little children came by. As they approached us he said to me:

"Watch the difference in these two boys."

Taking one of them in his arms he stood him on the gatepost, and stepping back a few feet he folded his arms and called to the little fellow to jump. In an instant the boy sprang toward him and was caught in his arms. Then turning to the second boy he tried the same experiment. But in the second case it was different. The child trembled and refused to move. My friend held out his arms and tried to induce the child to trust to his strength, but nothing could move him. At last my friend had to lift him down from the post and let him go.

"What makes such a difference in the two?" I asked.

My friend smiled and said, "The first is my own boy and knows me; but the other is a stranger's child whom I have never seen before."

There was all the difference. My friend was equally able to prevent both from falling, but the difference was in the boys themselves. The first had assurance in his father's ability and acted upon it, while the second, although he might have believed in the ability to save him from harm, would not put his belief into action.

So it is with us. We hesitate to trust ourselves to that loving One whose plans for us are far higher than any we have ourselves made. He, too, with outstretched arms, calls us, and would we but listen to His voice we would hear that invitation and promise of assurance as He gave it of old:

"Come unto Me, all ye that labor, and are heavy-laden, and I will give you rest."

Living Christ

Even though you cannot talk about Christ, you can live Him.

A young lady, a daughter of one of the wealthiest merchants in London, felt that she could not speak much for Christ, but I learned that every Sunday afternoon she stole out from that magnificent home of hers, and went to an old man who could not speak the English language, but could only speak Gaelic. This girl could read in that language, and every Sabbath afternoon she went and read to him, because that was the time of all the week when he was tempted to get drunk, and she wanted to save him.

Another case interested me very much. When I was in London, one of the wealthiest young men of the city, an only son of one of the leading London bankers, a young man who was coming into possession of millions, a student at Cambridge University, felt that he could not go into the inquiry meetings and work in that way, but he went out to a cabman one night and said:

"I will pay you your regular fee by the hour if you will go in and hear Mr. Moody preach. I will act as cabman and take care of your horse."

And on that cold, bleak night in London, that gentleman stood by the cabman's horse, and let that cabman go and hear the Gospel. He was gone about two hours, and all the while that young man stood there confessing Christ silently.

I said to a Scotchman one day as he stayed to the after-meeting, "Would you speak to that young man there?"

He was a great manufacturer. He said, "Mr. Moody, I am very reticent; I don't know that I could do that."

I said, "Perhaps you can help him; I wish you would speak to him."

He sat down beside the young man and found him to be a workingman. He said that every Saturday noon when he was paid off and went home to get his dinner, a terrible thirst for strong drink came on him, and that by Monday all his wages were drunk up.

This gentleman asked: "What time do you get your dinner?"

He told him. The next Saturday afternoon that great manufacturer was there, and spent the whole afternoon with him. The next Saturday he came again, and he kept at it until he got that man away from the power of strong drink.

That is a good way to confess Christ. If you can't do it with your lips, you can do it in some way. Watch for opportunities to let the world know on whose side you stand.

Garibaldi's Enthusiasm

I did not agree with Garibaldi's judgment in all things, but I did admire his enthusiasm. I never saw his name in the papers, or in a book, but I read all I could find about him. There was something about him that fired me up. I remember reading of the time when he was on the way to Rome in 1867, and when he was cast into prison. I read the letter he sent to his comrades:

"If fifty Garibaldis are thrown into prison, let Rome be free!"

He did not care for his own comfort, so long as the cause of freedom in Italy was advanced. If we have such a love for our Master and His cause that we are ready to go out and do His work whatever it may cost us personally, depend upon it the Lord will use us in building up His Kingdom.

A Typical Case

Experience has taught me that most of the men that talk against the Bible are men that never read it. There is no book in the world misjudged like the Bible. A modern book comes out, and people say:

"Have you read such a book?"

And you say, "Yes, I have just read it."

"Well, what is your opinion about it?"

"Well, I wouldn't like to give my opinion without reading it more carefully."

And yet men are very free to give their opinion about God's Book without reading it. A friend of mine was in Montreal some time ago, and he talked with a man upon the subject of Christ and Christianity.

"Well," he said, "the fact is we have got to have a new Bible. That old Book," he said, "was good enough for the Dark Ages, but we have outgrown it. It is of no use to this enlightened age."

My friend said, "Before we give up the old Book let us see how much we know about it. Can you tell me which is the first book in the Bible, Genesis or Revelation?"

Well, he said he couldn't just tell that. He didn't quite know, but he knew they had got to have another Bible.

That man is typical of all the men that I have ever heard howling and writing against the Bible. I never met one in my life—yes, I will make one exception, I did meet one man that claimed he had read it through; but I doubted him, because when I pressed him to quote something out of it all he could remember was "Jesus wept."

Everything Thrown Overboard

"There sometimes comes a time on shipboard when everything must be sacrificed to save the passengers. The cargo is thrown overboard, the rigging thrown away. At last the captain puts the trumpet to his lips, and shouts, 'Cut away the mast!'

"Some of you have been tossed and driven, and in your effort to keep the world, you have well nigh lost your soul. Overboard with all other anxieties and burdens! Drop the sails of pride and self righteousness! God will hear your faintest cry for help!"

The Love of God

Among the many victims of the Paris Commune was a Catholic bishop. He was a man who knew something of the love of God in his own experience. In the little cell where he was confined awaiting execution was a small window in the shape of a cross. After his death was found written above the cross, "height"; below it, "depth"; and at the end of each arm of the cross, "length" and "breadth." He had learned that God's love was unfailing in the hour of adversity and death.

Calling a Spade a Spade

A lady once said to me, "I have got so in the habit of exaggerating that my friends accuse me of exaggerating so that they don't understand me."

She said, "Can you help me? What can I do to overcome it?"

"Well," I said, "the next time you catch yourself lying, go right to that party and say you have lied, and tell him you are sorry. Say it is a lie; stamp it out, root and branch; that is what you want to do."

"Oh," she said, "I wouldn't like to call it *lying*."

But that is what it was. Christianity isn't worth a snap of your finger if it doesn't straighten out your character.

"I Ain't No Beggar!"

Mr. Morehouse once used an illustration which fastened itself on my mind. He said:

Suppose you go up the street and meet a man whom you have known for the last ten years to be a beggar, and you notice a change in his appearance, and you say:

"Hello, beggar, what's come over you?"

"I ain't no beggar. Don't call me a beggar."

"Why," you say, "I saw you the other day begging in the street."

"Ah, but a change has taken place," he replies.

"Is that so? how did it come about?"

"Well," he says, "I came out this morning, and got down here intending to catch the business men and get money out of them, when one of them came up to me and said there was $10,000 deposited for me in bank."

"How do you know this is true?" you say.

"I went to the bank and they put the money in my hand."

"Are you sure of that?" you ask; "how do you know it was the right kind of a hand?"

But he says: "I don't care whether it was the right

kind of a hand or not; I got the money, and that's all I wanted."

Faith is the hand that reaches out and takes the blessing. Any faith that brings you to Christ is the right kind of faith, and instead of looking at your faith look to Christ. See if you have the right kind of a Christ—a Christ that is giving you victory over sin. Faith is to the soul what the eye is to the body. I do not pick my eyes out of my head every now and then to see if they are the right kind of eyes. Yet people are doing that with faith all the time.

Some one has said, faith sees a thing in God's hand, and says, "I will have it." Unbelief sees it there, and says, "God won't give it me." Look to God by faith now and have salvation.

A Remarkable Picture

Some years ago a remarkable picture was exhibited in London. As you looked at it from a distance, you seemed to see a monk engaged in prayer, his hands clasped, his head bowed. As you came nearer, however, and examined the painting more closely, you saw that in reality he was squeezing a lemon into a punch bowl!

What a picture that is of the human heart! Superficially examined, it is thought to be the seat of all that is good and noble and pleasing in a man; whereas in reality, until regenerated by the Holy Ghost, it is the seat of all corruption. "This is the condemnation, that light is come into the world, and men *loved darkness rather than light.*"

He Turned the Laugh

A young man was preaching on the streets in London when an infidel came up and said:

"The man who invented gas did more for the world than Jesus Christ."

The young man could not answer him, and the crowd had the laugh on him. But another man got up and said:

"Of course the man has a right to his opinion, and I suppose if he was dying he would send for the gasfitter, but I think I should send for a minister and have him read the 14th chapter of John"; and he turned the laugh back on the man.

I Must Get on Board

I believe that the Cunard Line of steamers is a good line, and that if I should get on board of one of them next week, I should arrive in England in six or eight days. But if I did not get on board, I should not get there any more than one who did not believe so at all. We want a laying-hold belief. God offers Christ; we want not only to *believe* that, but to *take* Him. The Old Testament word for belief is trust. Isaiah xxvi:3, says: "Thou wilt keep him in perfect peace whose mind is stayed on Thee, because he trusteth in Thee."

Give Up Now!

Dr. Andrew Bonar told me how, in the Highlands of Scotland, a sheep would often wander off into the rocks and get into places that they couldn't get out of. The grass on these mountains is very sweet and the sheep like it, and they will jump down ten or twelve feet, and then they can't jump back again, and the shepherd hears them bleating in distress. They may be there for days, until they have eaten all the grass. The shepherd will wait until they are so faint they cannot stand, and then they will put a rope around him, and he will go over and pull that sheep up out of the jaws of death.

"Why don't they go down there when the sheep first gets there?" I asked.

"Ah!" he said, "they are so very foolish they would dash right over the precipice and be killed if they did!"

And that is the way with men; they won't go back to God till they have no friends and have lost everything. If you are a wanderer I tell you that the Good Shepherd will bring you back the moment you have given up trying to save yourself and are willing to let Him save you His own way.

The Popular Kind of Preaching

A young minister took a church in Scotland, and began to preach about the sins of the present day, and those of the people who came to hear him. The old sexton came to him and said:

"Young man, if you expect to hold this people you must be careful about preaching on modern sins. You can preach about the sins of Abraham, and Isaac, and Jacob, and the old Patriarchs, but don't you preach about the sins of the present day, because the people will not stand it."

"They Love a Fellow There!"

Show me a church where there is love, and I will show you a church that is a power in the community. In Chicago a few years ago a little boy attended a Sunday-school I know of. When his parents moved to another part of the city the little fellow still attended the same Sunday-school, although it meant a long, tiresome walk each way. A friend asked him why he went so far, and told him that there were plenty of others just as good nearer his home.

"They may be as good for others, but not for me," was his reply.

"Why not?" she asked.

"Because they love a fellow over there," he replied.

If only we could make the world believe that we loved them there would be fewer empty churches, and a smaller proportion of our population who never darken a church door. Let love replace duty in our church relations, and the world will soon be evangelized.

How to Kill Jealousy

There were two business men—merchants—and there was great rivalry between them, a great deal of bitter feeling. One of them was converted. He went to his minister and said:

"I am still jealous of that man, and I do not know how to overcome it."

"Well," he said, "if a man comes into your store to buy goods, and you cannot supply him, just send him over to your neighbor."

He said he wouldn't like to do that.

"Well," the minister said, "you do it, and you will kill jealousy."

He said he would, and when a customer came into his store for goods which he did not have, he would tell him to go across the street to his neighbor's. By and by the other began to send his customers over to this man's store, and the breach was healed.

The Unerring Guide

I am told by people who have been over the Alps, that the guide fastens them, if they are going in a dangerous place, right to himself, and he goes on before; they are fastened to the guide. And so should the Christian be linked to his unerring Guide, and be safely upheld.

If a man was going through the Mammoth Cave, it would be almost death to him if he strayed away from his guide—if separated from him, he would almost certainly perish. There are pitfalls in that cave, and a bottomless river, and there would be no chance for a man to find his way out of that cave without a guide or a light. So there is no chance for us to get through the dark wilderness of this world alone. It is folly for men and women to think that they can get through this evil world without the light of God's Word and the guidance of the Divine Spirit. God sent Him to guide us through this great journey, and if we seek to work independent of Him, we shall stumble into the deep darkness of eternity's night.

The Second Plan Succeeded

A young man enlisted, and was sent to his regiment. The first night he was in the barracks with about fifteen other young men, who passed the time playing cards and gambling. Before retiring, he fell on his knees and prayed, and they began to curse him and jeer at him and throw boots at him.

So it went on the next night and the next, and finally the young man went and told the chaplain what had taken place, and asked what he should do.

"Well," said the chaplain, "you are not at home now, and the other men have just as much right in the barracks as you have. It makes them mad to hear you pray, and the Lord will hear you just as well if you say your prayers in bed and don't provoke them."

For weeks after the chaplain did not see the young man again, but one day he met him, and asked—

"By the way, did you take my advice?"

"I did, for two or three nights."

"How did it work?"

"Well," said the young man, "I felt like a whipped hound, and the third night I got out of bed, knelt down and prayed."

"Well," asked the chaplain, "how did that work?"

The young soldier answered: "We have a prayer-meeting there now every night, and three have been converted, and we are praying for the rest."

Oh, friends, I am so tired of weak Christianity. Let us be out and out for Christ; let us give no uncertain sound. If the world wants to call us fools, let them do it. It is only a little while; the crowning day is coming. Thank God for the privilege we have of confessing Christ.

God Had Moved Him

There was an ex-judge in Chicago who thought that requests for prayer were too sacred to be made public, and he disliked my way of asking God's aid for those in need. He had a son who was with Grant at the seige of Richmond. One morning he became particularly depressed in spirit as his thoughts went out to the boy. He could not shake off the feeling that something was going to happen to his son, and he went to the meeting, and after much hesitation, asked me to pray for him. As he left the hall a telegram was handed to him. His son had been mortally wounded in battle that day. He said to me afterward that he firmly believed God put it into his head to come and ask for prayer.

Lies Never Called Back

The most dangerous thing about a lie is that a word once uttered can never be obliterated. Some one has said that lying is a worse crime than counterfeiting. There is some hope of following up bad coins until they are all recovered; but an evil word can never be overtaken. The mind of the hearer or reader has been poisoned, and human devices cannot reach in and cleanse it. Lies can never be called back.

A woman who was well known as a scandal-monger, went and confessed to the priest. He gave her a ripe thistle-top and told her to go out and scatter the seeds one by one. She wondered at the penance, but obeyed; then she came and told the priest. He next told her to go and gather again the scattered seeds. Of course she saw that it was impossible. The priest used it as an object-lesson to cure her of the sin of scandalous talk.

"More to Follow"

Rowland Hill used to tell a good story of a rich man and a poor man in his congregation. The rich man desired to do an act of benevolence, and so he sent a sum of money to a friend to be given to this poor man as he thought best. The friend just sent him five pounds, and said in the note:

"This is thine. Use it wisely. There is more to follow."

After a while he sent another five pounds, and said, "more to follow."

Again and again he sent the money to the poor man, always with the cheering words, "more to follow."

So it is with the wonderful grace of God. There is always "more to follow."

How to Repay a Good Deed

After the big Chicago fire I came to New York for money, and I heard there was a rich man in Fall River who was very liberal. So I went to him. He gave me a check for a large amount, and then got into his carriage and drove with me to the houses of other rich men in the city, and they all gave me checks. When he left me at the train I grasped his hand and said:

"If you ever come to Chicago, call on me, and I will return your favor."

He said: "Mr. Moody, don't wait for me; do it to the first man that comes along."

I never forget that remark; it had the ring of the true good Samaritan.

They Are Old Enough

I have no sympathy with the idea that our children have to grow up before they are converted. Once I saw a lady with three daughters at her side, and I stepped up to her and asked her if she was a Christian.

"Yes, sir."

Then I asked the oldest daughter if she was a Christian. The chin began to quiver, and the tears came into her eyes, and she said:

"I wish I was."

The mother looked very angrily at me and said, "I don't want you to speak to my children on that subject. They don't understand." And in great rage she took them all away from me. One daughter was fourteen years old, one twelve, and the other ten, but they were not old enough to be talked to about religion! Let them drift into the world and plunge into worldly amusements, and then see how hard it is to reach them. Many a mother is mourning to-day because her boy has gone beyond her reach, and will not allow her to pray with him. She may pray *for* him, but he will not let her pray or talk *with* him. In those early days when his mind was tender and young, she might have led him to Christ. Bring them in. "Suffer the little children to come unto Me."

Is there a prayerless father reading this? May God let the arrow go down into your soul! Make up your mind that, God helping you, you will get the children converted. God's order is to the father first, but if he isn't true to his duty, then the mother should be true, and save the children from the wreck. Now is the time to do it while you have them under your roof. Exert your parental influence over them.

What Made Both Safe

Some one has said that a little fly in Noah's ark was just as safe as an elephant. It was not the elephant's size and strength that made him safe. It was the ark that saved both elephant and fly.

It is not your righteousness, your good works, that will save you. Rich or poor, learned or unlearned, you can be saved only by the blood of Christ.

It Was Not Safe

There is a story of Doctor Chalmers. A lady came to him and said:

"Doctor, I cannot bring my child to Christ. I've talked, and talked, but it's of no use."

The doctor thought she had not much skill, and said, "Now you be quiet, and I will talk to her alone."

When he got the girl alone he said to her: "They are bothering you a good deal about this question; now suppose I just tell your mother you don't want to be talked to any more upon this subject for a year. How will that do?"

Well, the Scotch lassie hesitated a little, and then said she, "didn't think it would be safe to wait for a year. Something might turn up. She might die before then."

"That's so," replied the doctor; "but suppose we say six months."

She didn't think even this would be safe.

"Well, let us say three months," was the doctor's reply.

After a little hesitation, the girl finally said, "I don't think it would be safe to put it off for three months—don't think it would be safe to put it off at all," and they went down on their knees and she found Christ.

A Penalty Necessary

A person once said to me: "I hate your God; your God demands blood. I don't believe in such a God. My God is merciful to all. I do not know your God."

If you will turn to Lev. xvii. 11, you will find why God demands blood: "For the life of the flesh is in the blood; and I have given it to you upon the altar to make an atonement for your souls; for it is the blood that maketh an atonement for the soul."

Suppose there was a law that man should not steal, but no penalty was attached to stealing; some man would have my pocketbook before dinner. If I threatened to have him arrested, he would snap his fingers in my face. He would not fear the law, if there was no penalty. It is not the law that people are afraid of; it is the penalty attached.

Do you suppose God has made a law without a penalty. What an absurd thing it would be! Now, the penalty for sin is death: "the soul that sinneth, it shall die." I must die, or get somebody to die for me. If the Bible doesn't teach that, it doesn't teach anything. And that is where the atonement of Jesus Christ comes in.

Hard to be Counterfeited

A man can counterfeit love, he can counterfeit faith, he can counterfeit hope and all the other graces, but it is very difficult to counterfeit humility. You soon detect mock humility. They have a saying in the East among the Arabs, that as the tares and the wheat grow they show which God has blessed. The ears that God has blessed bow their heads and acknowledge every grain, and the more fruitful they are the lower their heads are bowed. The tares which God has sent as a curse, lift up their heads erect, high above the wheat, but they are only fruitful of evil. I have a pear-tree on my farm which is very beautiful; it appears to be one of the most beautiful trees on my place. Every branch seems to be reaching up to the light and stands almost like a wax candle, but I never get any fruit from it. I have another tree, which was so full of fruit last year that the branches almost touched the ground. If we only get down low enough, my friends, God will use every one of us to His glory.

"As the lark that soars the highest builds her nest the lowest; as the nightingale that sings so sweetly sings in the shade when all things rest; as the branches that are most laden with fruit bend lowest; as the ship most laden sinks deepest in the water; so the holiest Christians are the humblest."

The *London Times* some years ago told the story of a petition that was being circulated for signatures. It was a time of great excitement, and this petition was intended to have great influence in the House of Lords; but there was one word left out. Instead of reading, "We humbly beseech thee," it read, "We beseech thee." So it was ruled out. My friends, if we want to make an appeal to the God of heaven, we must humble ourselves; and if we do humble ourselves before the Lord, we shall not be disappointed.

Into the Lion's Mouth

A gentleman once went to Dr. Somerville, and said: "My son is going away to South America. He will not be within reach of the ordinances of religion. I know he will have no Sabbath; and he is to be away three years. Now, I want you to pray for him, that he may not lose all the good disposition he seems to feel."

Doctor Somerville looked at him and said: "Ay, you are going to put your son's head into the mouth of a lion, and then going to stand and pray, 'May the lion not crush him!'"

A Prayer-Meeting in Hell!

An aged minister fancied that he had committed the unpardonable sin. At last, after much conflict, he submitted to what he mistakably considered was the will of God, for him to be lost. Then something within him whispered:

"Suppose there is a hell for you, what would you, with your disposition and habits, do there?"

The quick answer was, "I would set up a prayer-meeting," and with the words came the light of God to show him the absurdity of it all. The fact that one fears that he has committed this sin is the sure proof that he has not.

As Others See Us

Leech, the celebrated artist and caricaturist, is said to have had an effective method of reprimanding his children. If their faces were distorted by anger, by a rebellious temper, or a sullen mood, he took out his sketch-book, transferred their lineaments to paper, and showed them, to their confusion, how ugly naughtiness was. Grown-up people like quite as little as children to see themselves as others see them. And yet, whether we like it or not, all our words and deeds are set down in God's book of remembrance.

A Grand Confession

I remember some meetings being held in a locality where the tide did not rise very quickly, and bitter and reproachful things were being said about the work. But one day, one of the most prominent men in the place rose and said:

"I want it to be known that I am a disciple of Jesus Christ; and if there is any odium to be cast on his cause, I am prepared to take my share of it."

It went through the meeting like an electric current, and a blessing came at once to his own soul and to the souls of others.

Best of All

A Jewish rabbi once asked his scholars what was the best thing a man could have in order to keep him in the straight path. One said *a good disposition;* another, *a good companion;* another said *wisdom* was the best thing he could desire. At last a scholar replied that he thought *a good heart* was best of all.

"True," said the rabbi, "you have comprehended all that the others have said. For he that hath a good heart will be of a good disposition, and a good companion, and a wise man. Let every one, therefore, cultivate a sincerity and uprightness of heart at all times, and it will save him an abundance of sorrow."

We need to make the prayer of David—"Create in me a clean heart, O God, and renew a right spirit within me!"

Only One Answer to This

If God put Adam out of the earthly Eden on account of one sin, do you think He will let us into the paradise above with tens of thousands of our sins upon us?

A Beautiful Legend

There is a beautiful tradition connected with the site on which the temple of Solomon was erected. It is said to have been occupied in common by two brothers, one of whom had a family, the other had none. On this spot was sown a field of wheat. On the evening succeeding the harvest—the wheat having been gathered in separate shocks—the elder brother said to his wife:

"My younger brother is unable to bear the burden and heat of the day; I will arise, take of my shocks and place with his without his knowledge."

The younger brother being actuated by the same benevolent motives, said within himself:

"My elder brother has a family, and I have none. I will arise, take of my shocks, and place them with his."

Judge of their mutual astonishment, when, on the following day, they found their respective shocks undiminished. This transpired for several nights, when each resolved in his own mind to stand guard and solve the mystery. They did so; and on the following night they met each other half-way between their respective shocks with their arms full. Upon ground hallowed by such associations as this was the temple of Solomon erected— so spacious and magnificent—the wonder and admiration of the world! Alas! in these days, how many would sooner steal their brother's whole shock than add to it a single sheaf!

Not Wanted

A man said to me some time ago: "Mr. Moody, now that I am converted, have I to give up the world?"

"No," said I, "you haven't to give up the world. If you give a good ringing testimony for the Son of God, the world will give you up pretty quick; they won't want you."

All Arranged Nicely

I got hold of an infidel some time ago. I said:

"How do you account for the formation of the world?"

"Oh! force and matter work together, and by chance the world was created."

I said: "It is a singular thing that your tongue isn't on the top of your head if force and matter just threw it together in that manner."

If I should take out my watch and say that force and matter worked together, and out came the watch, you would say I was a lunatic of the first order. Wouldn't you? And yet they say that this old world was made by chance! "It threw itself together!"

I met a man in Scotland, and he took the ground that there was no God. I asked him:

"How do you account for creation, for all these rocks?" (They have a great many rocks in Scotland.)

"Why!" he said, "any school boy could account for that."

"Well, how was the first rock made?"

"Out of sand."

"How was the first sand made?"

"Out of rock."

You see he had it all arranged so nicely. Sand and rock, rock and sand.

"Saved!"

At the time of the loss of the *Atlantic* on the banks of Newfoundland a business man was reported lost. His store was closed, and all his friends mourned for him as among those who went down on that vessel. But a telegram was received from him by his partner with the word "Saved," and that partner was filled with joy. The store was opened and the telegram was framed, and if you go into that store to-day you will see that little bit of paper hanging on the wall, with the word "Saved" upon it.

Let the news go over the wires to heaven to-day from you. Let the word "Saved" go from every one of you, and there will be joy in heaven. You can be saved—the Son of Man wants to save you.

Holding Church in a Saloon

When I first began to work for God in Chicago a Boston business man was converted there and stayed three months, and when leaving he said to me that there was a man living on such a street in whom he was very much interested, and whose boy was in the high school, and he had said that he had two brothers and a little sister who didn't go anywhere to Sabbath School, because their parents would not let them. This gentleman said:

"I wish you would go round and see them."

I went, and I found that the parents lived in a drinking saloon, and that the father kept the bar. I stepped up to him and told him what I wanted, and he said he would rather have his sons become drunkards and his daughter a harlot than have them go to our schools. It looked pretty dark, and he was very bitter to me, but I went a second time, thinking that I might catch him in a better humor. He ordered me out again. I went a third time and found him in better humor. He said:

"You are talking too much about the Bible. I will tell you what I will do; if you teach them something reasonable, like 'Paine's Age of Reason,' they may go."

Then I talked further to him, and finally he said: "If you will read Paine's book, I will read the New Testament."

Well, to get hold of him I promised, and he got the best of the bargain. We exchanged books, and that gave me a chance to call again and talk with that family.

One day he said: "Young man, you have talked so much about church, now you can have a church down here."

"What do you mean?"

"Why, I will invite some friends, and you can come down here and preach to them; not that I believe a word you say, but I do it to see if it will do us chaps any good."

"Very well," I said; "now let us have it distinctly understood that we are to have a certain definite time."

He told me to come at 11 o'clock, saying, "I want you to understand that you are not to do all the preaching."

"How is that?"

"I shall want to talk some, and also my friends."

I said, "Supposing we have it understood that you are to have forty-five minutes and I fifteen; is that fair?"

He thought that was fair. He was to have the first forty-five, and I the last fifteen minutes. I went down, and the saloonkeeper wasn't there. I thought perhaps he had backed out, but I found the reason was that he had found that his saloon was not large enough to hold all his friends, and he had gone to a neighbor's, whither I went and found two rooms filled. There were atheists, infidels and scoffers there. I had taken a little boy with me, thinking he might aid me. The moment I got in they plied me with all sorts of questions, but I said I hadn't come to hold any discussion; that they had been discussing for years and had reached no conclusion. They took up the forty-five minutes of time talking, and the result was there were no two who could agree.

Then came my turn. I said: "We always open our meetings with prayer; let us pray." I prayed, and thought perhaps some one else would pray before I got through. After I finished the little boy prayed. I wish you could have heard him. He prayed to God to have mercy upon those men who were talking so against His beloved Son. His voice sounded more like an angel's than a human voice. After we got up, I was going to speak, but there was not a dry eye in the assembly. One after another went out, and the old man I had been after for months—and sometimes it looked pretty dark—came and, putting his hands on my shoulder with tears streaming down his face, said:

"Mr. Moody, you can have my children go to your Sunday School."

The next Sunday they came, and after a few months the oldest boy, a promising young man then in the high school, came upon the platform; and with his chin quivering and the tears in his eyes, said: "I wish to ask these people to pray for me; I want to become a Christian."

God heard and answered our prayers for him. In all my acquaintances I don't know of a man whom it seemed more hopeless to reach. I believe if we lay ourselves out for the work there is not a man but can be reached and saved. I don't care who he is, if we go in the name of our Master, and persevere until we succeed, it will not be long before Christ will bless us, no matter how hard their heart is. "We shall reap if we faint not."

Faith Little, but God Great

A Scotch woman was once introduced as "Mrs. ——, a woman of great faith."

"No," she said, "I am a woman of little faith, but with a great God."

The Echo

You may have heard of the boy whose home was in a wood. One day he thought he heard the voice of another boy not far off. He shouted, "Hallo, there!" and the voice shouted back, "Hallo, there!" He did not know that it was the echo of his own voice, and he shouted again: "You are a mean boy!" Again the cry came back, "You are a mean boy!"

After some more of the same kind of thing he went into the house and told his mother that there was a bad boy in the wood. His mother, who understood how it was, said to him:

"Oh, no! You speak kindly to him, and see if he does not speak kindly to you."

He went to the wood again and shouted; "Hallo, there!" "Hallo, there!" "You are a good boy." Of course the reply came, "You are a good boy." "I love you." "I love you," said the other voice.

This little story explains the secret of the whole thing. Some of you perhaps think you have bad and disgreeable neighbors; most likely the trouble is with yourself. If you love your neighbors they will love you. Love begets love.

He Took the Prince at His Word

It is recorded in history that some years ago a man was condemned to be put to death. When he came to lay his head on the block, the prince who had charge of the execution asked him if there was any one petition that he could grant him. All that the condemned man asked for was a glass of water. They went and got him a tumbler of water, but his hand trembled so that he could not get it to his mouth.

The prince said to him, "Your life is safe until you drink that water."

He took the prince at his word, and dashed the water to the ground. They could not gather it up, and so he saved his life. My friend, you can be saved now by taking God at His Word. The water of life is offered to "whosoever will." Take it now, and live.

Another Kind of Pardon

During the war a boy in Pennsylvania was condemned to death. The boy expected to be pardoned and was resting upon that hope. The papers were full of statements that Governor Curtin would pardon the boy. One day Governor Curtin met Mr. George H. Stuart, the noted philanthropist, on the street, and said:

"Stuart, you know this boy who is sentenced to death. He is entertaining a hope that I am going to pardon him, and I can't do it. Now, go and tell him."

Mr. Stuart afterward told me that it was the hardest duty he had ever performed, but it was an act of mercy. When he entered the cell the prisoner rushed to him and cried:

"Mr. Stuart, you are a good man; I know you bring me a pardon."

Mr. Stuart knew not what to answer, but he summoned courage and told the boy the truth. The boy fell in a faint at Mr. Stuart's feet when he found his false hope taken away, but it prepared the way to tell him where alone a true and lasting hope might be found.

Drawing Daily

A man can no more take in a supply of grace for the future than he can eat enough to-day to last him for the next six months; or take sufficient air into his lungs at once to sustain life for a week to come. We must draw upon God's boundless stores of grace from day to day, as we need it.

"For Charlie's Sake"

Some years ago at a convention, an old judge was telling about the mighty power Christians summon to their aid in this petition "for Christ's sake!" "in Jesus' name!" and he told a story that made a great impression on me.

When the war came on, he said, his only son left for the army, and he became suddenly interested in soldiers. Every soldier that passed by brought his son to remembrance; he could see his son in him. He went to work for soldiers. When a sick soldier came there to Columbus one day, so weak he couldn't walk, the judge took him in a carriage, and got him into the Soldiers' Home. Soon he became president of the Soldiers' Home in Columbus, and used to go down every day and spend hours in looking after those soldiers, and seeing that they had every comfort. He spent on them a great deal of time and a great deal of money.

One day he said to his wife: "I'm giving too much time to these soldiers. I've got to stop it. There's an important case coming on in court, and I've got to attend to my own business."

He said he went down to the office that morning, resolved in future to let the soldiers alone. He went to his desk, and then to writing. Pretty soon the door opened, and he saw a soldier hobble slowly in. He started at sight of him. The man was fumbling at something in his breast, and pretty soon he got out an old soiled paper. The father saw it was his own son's writing.

"DEAR FATHER:—This young man belongs to my company. He has lost his leg and his health in defense of his country, and he is going home to his mother to die. If he calls on you, treat him kindly, FOR CHARLIE'S SAKE."

"For Charlie's sake." The moment he saw that, a pang went to his heart. He sent for a carriage, lifted the maimed soldier in, drove home, put him into Charlie's room, sent for the family physician, kept him in the family and treated him like his own son. When the young soldier got well enough to go to the train to go home to his mother, he took him to the railway station, put him in the nicest, most comfortable place in the carriage, and sent him on his way.

"I did it," said the old judge, "for Charlie's sake."

Now, whatsoever you do, my friends, do it for the Lord Jesus' sake. Do and ask everything in the name of Him "who loved us and gave Himself for us."

No Warmth in this Subject

During the time of slavery, a slave was preaching with great power. His master heard of it, and sent for him, and said:

"I understand you are preaching?"

"Yes," said the slave.

"Well, now," said the master, "I will give you all the time you need, and I want you to prepare a sermon on the Ten Commandments, and to bear down especially on stealing, because there is a great deal of stealing on the plantation."

The slave's countenance fell at once. He said he wouldn't like to do that; there wasn't the warmth in that subject there was in others.

I have noticed that people are satisfied when you preach about the sins of the patriarchs, but they don't like it when you touch upon the sins of to-day.

About Forgiveness

"If we confess our sins, He is faithful and just to forgive us our sins, and to cleanse us from all unrighteousness." That is the difference between a believer and a non-believer. If we have confessed our sins, it is distrusting God not to believe that they are put away.

Suppose that I have a little boy, and when I go home he comes to me and says: "Papa, I did that naughty thing you told me not to do."

I see there are signs of contrition, and say: "I am sorry you did it, but I am thankful you confessed it. I forgive you."

He goes off lightly. He has been forgiven. But the next day he comes and says:

"Papa, do you know that yesterday while you were away I did that naughty thing that you told me not to do. I am very sorry. Won't you forgive me?"

I say, "My son, was not that forgiven yesterday?"

"Well," he says, "I wish you would forgive me again."

Don't you see how dishonoring it is? It is very disheartening to a father to have a child act in that way. And it is distrusting God, and dishonoring Him for us to be constantly lugging up the past. If God has forgiven us, that is the end of it. "Who will lay anything to the charge of God's elect? It is God that justifieth." If God has justified me, will He lay any charge against me? But, dear friend, if you are not already forgiven, do not sleep until you are. Have this question of sin forever settled for time and eternity. God wants to forgive you, and He will, if you will confess your sins and ask His pardon.

Not Ashamed of It

There is a story told of Carey, the great missionary, that he was invited by the Governor-General of India to go to a dinner party at which were some military officers belonging to the aristocracy, and who looked down upon missionaries with scorn and contempt.

One of these officers said at the table: "I believe that Carey was a shoemaker, wasn't he, before he took up the profession of a missionary?"

Mr. Carey spoke up and said: "Oh, no, I was only a cobbler. I could mend shoes, and wasn't ashamed of it."

Out of the Poorhouse

A few year ago, I was going away to preach one Sunday morning, when a young man drove up in front of us. He had an aged woman with him.

"Who is that young man?" I asked.

"Do you see that beautiful meadow?" said my friend, "and that land there with the house upon it?"

"Yes."

"His father drank that all up," said he; and he went on to tell me all about him. His father was a great drunkard, squandered his property, died and left his wife in the poorhouse. "And that young man is one of the finest young men I ever knew. He has toiled hard and earned money, and bought back the land; he has taken his mother out of the poorhouse, and now he is taking her to church."

I thought, that is an illustration for me. The first Adam in Eden sold us for naught, but the Messiah, the second Adam, came and bought us back again. The first Adam brought us to the poorhouse, as it were; the second Adam makes us kings and priests unto God. That is redemption. We get in Christ all that Adam lost, and more. Men look on the blood of Christ with scorn and contempt, but the time is coming when the blood of Christ will be worth more than all the kingdoms of the world.

"The Precious Blood."

A lady came to me once when I was preaching some years ago in a western city, and asked me if I wouldn't talk to her husband; that when she spoke to him on religion he paid no attention, and she might as well talk to a post. I told her she had better pray God to convince and convict him.

They used to come to the meetings together, and often as I was speaking I would see her eyes close and her lips move, and I knew she was praying God to convict him. They came about a dozen times during the winter.

One night, after he had taken his seat, I noticed that his eyes looked as if he had been weeping. I gave out one hymn after another, all bearing on the Atonement, as that was the subject for the sermon. When I gave out the text, "The precious blood," I saw him cover his face and bow his head, and he fairly wept aloud. He followed me into the inquiry room after the meeting was over, and said to me:

"Mr. Moody, this has been the most extraordinary day in my life. When I got up this morning the words 'Precious blood' came into my mind. When I went down town to my place of business the words 'Precious blood' were ringing in my mind, and all during the day it was 'Precious blood, precious blood.' They followed me here to-night, and when you gave out your text, 'The precious blood,' I could hardly stay in my seat. I can't understand it."

"Well," I said, "I can"; and after talking with him for a while he accepted Christ then and there.

He is now dead, but when I was passing through that

city years after I asked about him, and they told me in all the years he had lived he had never lost his hold on Christ.

The Indians Could Understand That

Eternal life—there is no end to it! It is life without end. The government was trying to make a treaty with the Indians, and in one place put in the word "forever." The Indians did not like that word, and said:

"No; put it, 'As long as water runs and grass grows.'"

They could understand that. "The wages of sin is death; but the gift of God is eternal life."

Lots of People Like Him

A friend of mine told me some years ago that his wife was very fond of painting, but that for a long time he never could see any beauty in her paintings; they all looked like a daub to him. One day his eyes troubled him, and he went to see an oculist. The man looked in amazement at him, and said:

"You have what we call a short eye and a long eye, and that makes everything a blur."

He gave him some glasses that just fitted him, and then he could see clearly. Then he understood why it was that his wife was so carried away with art, and he went and built an art gallery, and filled it full of beautiful things, because everything looked so beautiful after he had had his eyes straightened out.

Now there are lots of people that have a long eye and a short eye, and they make miserable work of their Christian life. They keep one eye on the eternal city and the other eye on the well-watered plains of Sodom, and they have no happiness and enjoyment in either.

Sincerity v. Truth

Some people tell you it makes no difference what you believe, if you are only sincere. I have heard lots of people say, "You do not think it makes any difference what a man's creed is, do you, if he is only sincere? The disciples of Mahomet and Confucius are all right if they are only sincere."

That is the biggest lie that ever came out of hell. A lie never lifted any one yet. It is the truth that makes us free, and it is *that* which we want to believe. A lie does a man no good simply because he is sincere.

Suppose that I present a check for $10,000 at some bank, and the cashier says:

"Have you any money in this bank?"

I say, "No."

"Well," he says, "why are you trying to draw this money?"

I answer, "Well, I am very *sincere* about it, and I want $10,000 very much; I don't think any man wants it more than I do."

My earnestness will not get me that money. Some people get hold of a lie, and hold on to it. If you are wise, my friend, you will look and see if you believe the truth or not.

She Would Prefer Me

If my wife were in a foreign country, and I had a beautiful mansion all ready for her, she would a good deal rather I should come and bring her to it than to have me send some one else to bring her. Christ has prepared a mansion for His bride, the Church, and He promises for our joy and comfort that He will come Himself and bring us to the place He has been all this while preparing.

You Must Have Both

I believe in a faith that you can see, a living, working faith that prompts to action. Faith without works is like a man putting all his money into the foundation of a house; and works without faith is like building a house on sand without any foundation.

You often hear people say: "The root of the matter is in him." What would you say if I had a garden and nothing but roots in it? Suppose I hire two men to set out some trees, and at night I go to see how they are getting on. I find that one has set out a hundred trees, and the other only ten. The first man says to me:

"Look at my trees! Don't they look as well as that man's, and he has set out only ten?"

I say to the other: "How's this?"

"Well," he says, "wait a short time, and you will see how it is. That man doesn't believe in roots, and he has cut off the little roots and stuck the trees in like sticks. I have set out ten trees, roots and all."

What roots are to the tree, faith is to the child of God. If we are to have eternal life, if we are to bear fruit, we must be rooted and grounded in Christ Jesus.

It Becomes New

When I was in Baltimore last, my window looked out on an Episcopal Church. The stained glass windows were dull and uninviting by day, but when the lights shone through at night, how beautiful they were!

So when the Holy Spirit touches the eyes of your understanding, and you see Christ shining through the pages of the Bible, it becomes a new book to you.

Calling the Roll of Heaven

A soldier, wounded during our last war, lay dying in his cot. Suddenly the deathlike stillness of the room was broken by the cry, "Here! Here!" which burst from the lips of the dying man. Friends rushed to the spot and asked what he wanted.

"Hark," he said, "they are calling the roll of heaven, and I am answering to my name."

In a few moments once more he whispered, "Here!" and passed into the presence of the King.

The Light of Nature

"Men strike their knives into the Bible, and say the light of nature is sufficient. Indeed! Have the fire-worshippers of India, cutting themselves until blood spurts at every pore—have they found the light of nature sufficient? Has the Bornesian cannibal, gnawing the roasted flesh from human bones—has he found the light of nature sufficient? Has the Chinese woman, with her foot cramped and deformed into a hoof—has she found the light of nature sufficient? Could the ancients see heaven from the heights of Ida or Olympus? No! I call upon the pagodas of superstition, the tortures of Brahma, the infanticide of the Ganges, the bloody wheels of the Juggernaut, to prove that the light of nature is *not* sufficient. A star is beautiful, but it pours no light into the midnight darkness of a sinful soul. The flower is sweet, but it exudes no balm for the heart's wound."—[Talmage.]

A Good Word for the Devil

A child once said to his mother, "Mamma, you never speak ill of any one. You would speak well of Satan."

"Well," said the mother, "you might imitate his perseverance."

A Perfect Farce!

Professor Drummond once described a man going into one of our after-meetings and saying he wanted to become a Christian.

"Well, my friend, what is the trouble?"

He doesn't like to tell. He is greatly agitated. Finally he says, "The fact is, I have overdrawn my account"—a polite way of saying he has been stealing.

"Did you take your employer's money?"

"Yes."

"How much?"

"I don't know. I never kept account of it."

"Well, you have an idea you stole $1,500 last year?"

"I am afraid it is that much."

"Now, look here, sir, I don't believe in sudden work; don't steal more than a thousand dollars this next year, and the next year not more than five hundred, and in the course of the next few years you will get so that you won't steal any. If your employer catches you, tell him you are being converted; and you will get so that you won't steal any by and by."

My friends, the thing is a perfect farce! "Let him that stole, steal no more," that is what the Bible says. It is right about face.

Take another illustration. Here comes a man, and he admits that he gets drunk every week. That man comes to a meeting, and wants to be converted. Shall I say, "Don't you be in a hurry. I believe in doing the work gradually. Don't you get drunk and knock your wife down more than once a month?" Wouldn't it be refreshing to his wife to go a whole month without being knocked down? Once a month, only twelve times in a year! Wouldn't she be glad to have him converted in this new way! Only get drunk after a few years on the anniversary of your wedding, and at Christmas, and then it will be effective because it is gradual!

Oh! I detest all that kind of teaching. Let us go to the Bible and see what that old Book teaches. Let us believe it, and go and act as if we believed it, too. Salvation is instantaneous. I admit that a man may be converted so that he cannot tell when he crossed the line between death and life, but I also believe a man may be a thief one moment and a saint the next. I believe a man may be as vile as hell itself one moment, and be saved the next.

Christian growth is gradual, just as physical growth is; but a man passes from death unto everlasting life quick as an act of the will—"He that believeth on the Son *hath* everlasting life."

What Does He Want Most?

What does the hungry man want? Money? Not at all. Fame? No. Good clothes? Not a bit. He wants *food*. What does the thirsty man want? Reputation? Bonds and stocks? No! he wants water. When we are dead in earnest and want the bread of heaven and the water of life, we shall not stop till we get them.

"Give Him a Cheer!"

You have heard the story of the child who was rescued from the fire that was raging in a house away up in the fourth story. The child came to the window, and as the flames were shooting up higher and higher it cried out for help. A fireman started up the ladder of the fire-escape to rescue the child from its dangerous position. The wind swept the flames near him, and it was getting so hot that he wavered, and it looked as if he would have to return without the child. Thousands looked on, and their hearts quaked at the thought of the child having to perish in the fire, as it must do if the fireman did not reach it. Some one in the crowd cried:

"Give him a cheer!"

Cheer after cheer went up, and as the man heard them he gathered fresh courage. Up he went into the midst of the smoke and the fire, and brought down the child in safety.

If you cannot go and rescue the perishing yourself, you can at least pray for those who do, and cheer them on. If you do, the Lord will bless the effort. Do not grumble and criticise; it takes neither heart nor brains to do that.

Bankrupt Sinners are Scarce

Very few people think they are lost. You seldom meet a bankrupt sinner. Most of them think they can pay about seventy-five cents on the dollar; some ninety-nine per cent—they just come short a little, and the Almighty will make it up somehow.

Don't let Satan make you think you are so good that you don't need the grace of God. We are a bad lot, all of us.

Are *You* Sure?

After John Wesley had been preaching for some time, some one said to him, "Are you sure, Mr. Wesley, of your salvation?"

"Well," he answered, "Jesus Christ died for the whole world."

"Yes, we all believe that; but are you sure that *you* are saved?"

Wesley replied that he was sure that provision had been made for his salvation.

"But are you sure, Wesley, that *you* are saved?"

It went like an arrow to his heart, and he had no rest or power until that question was settled.

Many men and many women go on month after month, and year after year, without power, because they do not know their standing in Christ; they are not sure of their own footing for eternity. Latimer wrote Ridley once that when he was settled and steadfast about his own salvation he was as bold as a lion, but if that hope became eclipsed he was fearful and afraid and was disqualified for service. Many are disqualified for service because they are continually doubting their own salvation.

No Hypocrites in Heaven, Anyway!

"I won't become a Christian because of hypocrites in the churches." My friend, you will find very few there if you get to heaven. There won't be a hypocrite in the next world, and if you don't want to be associated with hypocrites in the next world, you will take this invitation. You find hypocrites everywhere! One of the apostles was himself the very prince of hypocrites, but he didn't get to heaven. You will find plenty of hypocrites in the church. They have been there for the last nineteen hundred years, and will probably remain there. But what is that to you? This is an individual matter between you and your God.

We Cannot Deceive God

The merchant's measure may be wrong, but God's measure is just and right. The merchant measures a gallon of oil or a pound of tea, and does not give full measure. God says to the recording angel:

"So many drops too few; so many grains short. Write it down.

We may cheat man, but we cannot cheat God.

How the Grumbler Was Cured

Some years ago, a pastor of a little church in a small town became exceedingly discouraged, and brooded over his trials to such an extent that he became an inveterate grumbler. He found fault with his brethren because he imagined they did not treat him well. A brother minister was invited to assist him a few days in a special service. At the close of the Sabbath morning service our unhappy brother invited the minister to his house to dinner. While they were waiting alone in the parlor he began his doleful story by saying:

"You have no idea of my troubles; and one of the greatest is that my brethren in the church treat me very badly."

The other propounded the following questions:

"Did they ever spit in your face?"

"No; they haven't come to that."

"Did they ever smite you?"

"No."

"Did they ever crown you with thorns?"

This last question he could not answer, but bowed his head thoughtfully. The other replied:

"Your Master and mine was thus treated, and all His disciples fled and left Him in the hands of the wicked. Yet He opened not His mouth."

The effect of this conversation was wonderful. Both ministers bowed in prayer and earnestly sought to possess the mind which was in Christ Jesus. During the ten days' meetings the discontented pastor became wonderfully changed. He labored and prayed with his friend, and many souls were brought to Christ.

Some weeks after, a deacon of the church wrote and said: "Your late visit and conversation with our pastor have had a wonderful influence for good. We never hear him complain now, and he labors more prayerfully and zealously.'

No Anxiety

Dr. Watts could say, "I bless God I can lie down with comfort to-night, not being anxious whether I wake in this world or in another."

"Are All the Children In!"

Some one sent me a paper a number of years ago containing an article that was marked. Its title was: "Are all the children in?" An old wife lay dying. She was nearly one hundred years of age, and the husband who had taken the journey with her, sat by her side. She was just breathing faintly, but suddenly she revived, opened her eyes, and said:

"Why! it is dark."

"Yes, Janet, it is dark."

"Is it night?"

"Oh, yes! it is midnight."

"Are all the children in?"

There was that old mother living life over again. Her youngest child had been in the grave twenty years, but she was traveling back into the old days, and she fell asleep in Christ, asking:

"Are all the children in?"

Dear friend, are they all in? Put the question to yourself now. Is John in? Is James in? Or is he immersed in business and pleasure? Is he living a double and dishonest life? Say! where is your boy, mother? Where is your son, your daughter? Is it well with your children? Can you say it is?

High Level Every Time

When I was in London I wanted to go to the Crystal Palace. When I went to buy my railway ticket the agent asked; "High level or low level?" Without thinking or knowing what he meant, I said:

"Low level."

When we got out at the grounds they landed us away down in a hollow, and I had to climb a number of steep steps. When I got to the top, all out of breath, I saw that if I had taken the high level, it would have landed me right in the palace. I've taken the "high level" ever since.

All Invited

A lady told me once that she was so hard-hearted she couldn't come to Christ.

"Well," I said, "my good woman, it doesn't say 'all ye soft-hearted people come.' Black hearts, vile hearts, hard hearts, soft hearts, all hearts come. Who can soften your hard heart but Himself?"

He Was Insincere

Some years ago I went into a man's house, and when I commenced to talk about religion he turned to his daughter and said:

"You had better leave the room. I want to say a few words to Mr. Moody."

When she had gone, he opened a perfect torrent of infidelity upon me.

"Why did you send your daughter out of the room before you said this?" I asked.

"Well," he replied, "I did not think it would do her any good to hear what I said."

Is his rock as our Rock? Would he have sent his daughter out if he really believed what he said?

"Dinna Ye Hear Them?"

During the Indian mutiny, the English were besieged in the city of Lucknow, and were in momentary expectation of perishing at the hands of the fiends that surrounded them. A little Scotch lassie was in this fort, and, while lying on the ground, she suddenly shouted, her face aglow with joy:

"Dinna ye hear them comin'? dinna ye hear them comin'?"

"Hear what?" they asked.

"Dinna ye hear them comin'?"

She sprang to her feet. It was the bagpipes of her native Scotland she heard. It was a native air she heard that was being played by a regiment of her countrymen marching to the relief of those captives, and these deliverers made them free.

Oh, friend, don't you hear the voice of Jesus Christ calling to you now?

A Good Definition

A Christian workingman, being asked by what means he kept walking in the paths of obedience, replied:

"Well, I came to the Saviour; He received Me; and I never said, 'good-bye.'"

In his Drawingroom

There was a young man in the middle west who had been more or less interested about his soul's salvation. One afternooon, in his office, he said:

"I will accept Jesus Christ as my Lord and Savior."

He went home and told his wife, who was a nominal professor of religion, that he had made up his mind to serve Christ, and he added:

"After supper to-night I am going to take the company into the drawing-room and erect the family altar."

"Well," said his wife, "you know some of the gentlemen who are coming to tea are skeptics, and they are older than you are, and don't you think you had better wait until after they have gone, or else go out in the kitchen and have your first prayer with the servants?"

The young man thought for a few moments, and then he said:

"I have asked Jesus Christ into my house for the first time, and I shall take Him into the best room, and not into the kitchen."

So he called his friends into the drawing-room. There was a little sneering, but he read and prayed. That man afterward became Chief Justice of the United States Court.

Never be ashamed of the Gospel of Christ; it is the power of God unto salvation.

Don't Give it Up

If you have a good excuse, don't give it up for anything I have said; don't give it up for anything your mother may have said; don't give it up for anything your friend may have said. Take it up to the bar of God and state it to Him. But if you have not got a good excuse—an excuse that will stand in eternity—let it go now and flee to the arms of a loving Savior.

The Life Beyond

There is a little book entitled "The Life Beyond" that presents the truth of the resurrection in a wonderful manner. It is an allegory, and pretends to give the experiences of a little dragon fly grub. The little insect longs to know what is beyond the sphere of its little world. In vain it inquires of the fish that live in the same pond, but they have no experience in any other sphere, nor can any of its fellows satisfy its anxious yearning. The only world it knows is a little meadow pond; all its experience is limited by the bounds of the surrounding banks.

At length the grub is overcome by a strange attraction upward, and gathering about it all its fellows it tells that it must leave them for the regions above, and promises to return to tell them what it has found to exist in the beyond, if, indeed, there may be anything above the bulrushes of their little pond. And then quietly it disappears from the sight of its fellows and emerges into the bright sunlight of the greater world. Here it is transformed, and with outstretched wings it darts hither and thither reflecting the brightness of the sun from its gorgeous body. But it does not forget the promises it has made to the friends it has left below. It tries to return to the world from which it has just risen, but cannot leave the atmosphere in which it lives. All it can do is to wait for them to come to where it now lives, a beautiful dragon fly.

And thus it is with those who have disappeared from our sight. Their love for us may not be lessened because they are not able to commune with us, but they are waiting in the presence of the Master for that glorious moment when in resurrected bodies they shall unite once more with us whom they have loved on earth.

Man's Idea of Grace

Men talk about grace, but, as a rule, they know very little about it. Let a business man go to one of your bankers to borrow a few hundred dollars for sixty or ninety days; if he is well able to pay, the banker will perhaps lend him the money if he can get another responsible man to sign the note with him. They give what they call "three days' grace" after the sixty or ninety days have expired; but they will make the borrower pay interest on the money during these three days, and if he does not return principal and interest at the appointed time, they will sell his goods; they will perhaps turn him out of his house, and take the last piece of furniture in his possession.

That is not grace at all; but that fairly illustrates man's idea of it. Grace not only frees you from payment of the interest, but of the principal also. The grace of God frees us from the penalty of our sin without any payment on our part. Christ has paid the debt, and all we have to do is to believe on Him for our salvation.

Across the River

A minister who had lost his child asked another minister to come and preach for him. He came and told how he lived on one side of a river, and felt very little interest in the people on the other side until his daughter was married and went over there to live. Then every morning he went to the window and looked over that river, and felt very much concerned about that town and all the people there.

"Now," said he, "I think that as this child has crossed another river, heaven will be dearer to my friend than ever it has been before."

A Difference in the Singing

I was in a town in the north of Scotland a good many years ago, where they sang nothing but the Psalms. They had a church that held the whole town of about two thousand five hundred people, and I think I never heard the Twenty-third Psalm sung as they sang it—"The Lord's my shepherd." It was grand singing. When I finished preaching, I said:

"I never heard the Twenty-third Psalm sung so well, and I wonder how many sang it from the heart. I should like to have all who can sing it from the heart rise and sing it again."

I never heard it sung so poorly. I do not think there were fifty people on their feet. It is one thing to sing, "The Lord is my shepherd," and it is another thing to believe it. Is the Lord really *your* shepherd?

They all Black-balled him

There was a sailor whose mother had long been praying for him. One night the memory of his mother came home to this man; he thought of the days of his childhood, and made up his mind he would try and lead a different life. When he got to New York he thought he would join the Odd Fellows; he imagined that would be a good way to begin. What miserable mistakes men make when they get trying to save themselves! This man applied to a lodge of Odd Fellows for admission; but the committee found that he was a drinking man, and so they black-balled him. Then he thought he would try the Free Masons; they discovered what sort of a man he was, and they black-balled him, too.

One day he was walking along Fulton street, when

he received an invitation to come to the daily prayer-meeting held there. He went in, and heard about the Savior; he received Christ into his heart, and found the peace and power he wanted. Some days after he stood up in the meeting and told his story—how the Odd Fellows had black-balled him; how the Free Masons had black-balled him; and how he came to the Lord Jesus Christ, who had not black-balled him, but took him right in.

That is what Christ will do to every penitent sinner. "This Man receiveth sinners." Come to Him to-day, and He will receive you; His marvelous, sovereign grace will cover and put away all your sins.

She Made a Mistake

Doctor Arnot was accustomed to tell a story of a poor woman who was in great distress because she could not pay her landlord his rent. The doctor put some money in his pocket, and went round to her house, intending to help her. When he got there he knocked at the door. He thought he heard some movement inside; but no one came to open the door. He knocked louder and louder still; but yet no one came. Finally he kicked at the door, causing some of the neighbors to look out and see what was going on, but he could get no entrance. At last he went away, thinking his ears must have deceived him, and that there was really no one there.

A day or two afterward he met the woman in the street, and told her what had happened. She held up her hands and exclaimed:

"Was that you? I was in the house all the while; but I thought it was the landlord, and I had the door locked!"

Many people think the grace of God is coming to smite them. My dear friends, it is coming to pay all your debts!

A Tragic Ending

At one place where I went to hold meetings it was advertised in the papers that I was going to stay thirty days. Now, there was a lady who was a member of one of the churches, and she said:

"I don't want to have my boy brought under the influence of those meetings. I'm afraid he'll be brought into the Young Men's Christian Association, and they'll have him out on the streets with tracts, and it would be very mortifying to me to have my son doing such a thing as that."

She was ambitious for her boy, and wanted to get him into the bon-ton society, as they call it. So she planned to take her son out of the city, and to be gone for those thirty days. She told her pastor why she had taken him, but I knew nothing about it.

The meetings went on, and just at my right hand sat that minister, from the beginning till the end, until the last meeting, when he was absent. Just as the benediction was pronounced, and the people were about to leave, he came rushing in, and said he was so sorry he had not been there.

"I have just been called on one of the saddest errands of my life," he said, and went on to tell me that that mother who had taken her son away from the influence of those meetings had brought him back that day in his coffin, and he had just come from the funeral.

A Temple of the Holy Ghost

Some men were burying an aged saint some time ago, and he was very poor, like many of God's people, poor in this world, but very rich in the other world, and they were just hastening him off to the grave, wanting to get rid of him, when an old minister, who was officiating at the grave, said:

"Tread softly, for you are carrying a temple of the Holy Ghost."

Whenever you see a believer, you see a temple of the Holy Ghost.

Polybius Opinion

Polybius says that whereas man is held to be the wisest of all creatures, to him he seems to be the most foolish. Where other creatures have smarted, they will come no more; the fox returns not to the snare, nor the wolf to the pitfall. But man returns to the same sins, and will not take warning until he is utterly ruined.

This Young Man Made a Mistake

In 1872, when I was coming back from Europe, there were a number of ministers on board. A young man who had evidently crossed several times before and knew the captain, stepped up to him, and in a loud tone of voice, intending doubtless to insult some of the ministers, said he was sorry he had taken passage on the boat, as it would be unlucky to travel with so many parsons. The captain was himself a pretty rough fellow, and turning to him he said:

"If you'll show me a town in England where there are five thousand people and not one parson, I'll show you a place a mile nearer hell than ever you've been."

The young man slunk away. I'd like to take all these people who do not believe in these things and put them on an island by themselves. Why, they'd sink the first boat that touched there in their efforts to get on board and get away!

"Sowing the Tares"

I was at the Paris Exhibition in 1867, and I noticed there a little oil painting, only about a foot square, and the face was the most hideous I have ever seen. On the paper attached to the painting were the words "Sowing the Tares." The face looked more like a demon's than a man's. As he sowed these tares, up came serpents and reptiles, and they were crawling up his body, and all around were woods with wolves and animals prowling in them. I have seen that picture many times since. Ah! the reaping time is coming. If you sow to the flesh you must reap corruption.

Turning on the Searchlight

When I was going through the land of Goshen in Egypt, a few years ago, as I came near the city of Alexandria, I saw the strangest sight I had ever seen. The heavens were lit up with a new kind of light, and there seemed to be flash after flash; I couldn't understand it. I had heard that the Khedive had died, and that a new Khedive was coming into power. I found later that England had sent over some war vessels, and the moment that darkness came on they had turned their searchlights upon that city; it was almost as light as noonday. Every street was lit up, and I do not suppose that ten men could have met in any part of Alexandria without being discovered by that searchlight.

May God turn His searchlight upon us, and see if there be any evil way in us!

Debts All Paid

Justification puts a man before God as if he had never sinned. God looks in His ledger, and says:

"Moody, your debts have all been paid by Another; there is nothing against you!"

She Didn't Know their Value

A poor old widow, living in the Scottish Highlands, was called upon one day by a gentleman who had heard that she was in need. The old lady complained of her condition, and remarked that her son was in Australia and doing well.

"But does he do nothing to help you?" inquired the visitor.

"No, nothing," was the reply. "He writes me regularly once a month, but only sends me a little picture with his letter."

The gentleman asked to see one of the pictures that she had received, and found each one of them to be a draft for ten pounds.

That is the condition of many of God's children. He has given us many "exceeding great and precious promises," which we either are ignorant of or fail to appropriate. Many of them seem to be pretty pictures of an ideal peace and rest, but are not appropriated as practical helps in daily life. And not one of these promises is more neglected than the assurance of salvation. An open Bible places them within reach of all, and we may appropriate the blessing which such a knowledge brings.

They Did Not Heed the Signal

I was in the north of England in 1881, when a fearful storm swept over that part of the country. A friend of mine, who was a minister at Eyemouth, had a great many of the fishermen of the place in his congregation. It had been very stormy weather, and the fishermen had been detained in the harbor for a week. One day, however, the sun shone out in a clear blue sky; it seemed as if the storm had passed away, and the boats started out for the fishing-ground. Forty-one boats left the harbor that day. Before they started, the harbor-master hoisted the storm signal, and warned them of the coming tempest. He begged of them not to go; but they disregarded his warning, and away they went. They saw no sign of the coming storm. In a few hours, however, it swept down on that coast, and very few of those fishermen returned. There were five or six men in each boat, and nearly all were lost in that dreadful gale. In the church of which my friend was pastor, I believe there were three male members left.

Those men were ushered into eternity because they did not give heed to the warning. I lift up the storm-signal now, and warn you to escape from the coming judgment!

Reaped as He Sowed

A leading surgeon performed a critical operation before his class one day. The operation was successful, as far as his part was concerned. But he turned to the class and said:

"Six years ago a wise way of living might have prevented this disease. Two years ago a safe and simple operation might have cured it. We have done our best to-day as the case now stands, but Nature will have her word to say. She does not always repeal her capital sentences."

Next day the patient died, reaping the fruit of his excesses

"Ye Are My Witnesses"

A friend of mine in Philadelphia was going by a drinking saloon one night, and he saw in that saloon a professed Christian playing cards. He took a pencil, wrote on a card, and saw a little boy and said:

"My boy, here is some money. I want you to do an errand for me. You see that man on the side of the table where those three are, playing cards with them?"

"Yes, I do."

"Well," said my friend, "take that card to him."

The boy went in, and my friend watched the man when this card was handed to him. What was written on the card was, "Ye are my witnesses." The man took the card, looked at it, sprang to his feet, and rushing out into the street asked the boy where the card came from. The boy said:

"A man over there gave it to me."

But the man had slipped away. "Ye are my witnesses." Wherever you find a professed Christian going in bad company, you may look for something worse.

"I Died Trusting in Jesus!"

After the terrible battle of Pittsburgh Landing, we were taking the wounded down the Tennessee river to hospital. I said to some of the Christian Commission workers who were with me:

"We must not let a man die on this boat without telling him of Christ and heaven."

You know the cry of a wounded man is "Water! water!" As we passed along from one to another giving them water, we tried to tell them of the water of life, of which if they would drink they would never die. I came to one man who had about as fine a face as I ever saw. I spoke to him, but he did not answer. I went to the doctor, and said:

"Doctor, do you think that man will recover?"

"No; he lost so much blood before we got him off the field that he fainted while we were amputating his leg. He will never recover."

I said: "I can't find out his name, and it seems a pity to let him die without knowing who he is. Don't you think we can bring him to?"

"You may give him a little brandy and water," said the doctor; "that will revive him if anything will."

I sat down beside him, and gave him brandy and water every now and then. While I was waiting, I said to a man near by:

"Do you know this man?"

"Oh, yes; that is my chum."

"Has he a father and mother living?"

"He has a widowed mother."

"Has he any brothers or sisters?"

"Two sisters; but he is the only son."

"What is his name?"

"William Clark."

I said to myself that I could not let him die without getting a message for that mother. Presently he opened his eyes, and I said:

"William, do you know where you are?"

He looked around a little dazed, and then said: "Oh, yes; I am on my way home to mother."

"Yes, you are on your way home," I said; "but the doctor says you won't reach your earthly home. I thought I'd like to ask you if you had any message for your mother."

His face lighted up with an unearthly glow, as he

said: "Oh, yes; tell my mother that I died trusting in Jesus!"

It was one of the sweetest things I ever heard in my life!

Presently I said: "Anything else, William?"

With a beautiful smile he said: "Tell my mother and sisters to be sure to meet me in heaven"; and he closed his eyes.

He was soon unconscious again, and in a few hours his soul took its flight to join his Lord and Master.

Ruling by Love

In the little country district where I went to school there were two parties. One party said that boys could not possibly be controlled without the cane, and they kept a schoolmaster who acted on their plan; the other party said they should be controlled by love. The struggle went on, and at last, on one election day, the first party was put out, and the other ruled in their stead. I happened to be at the school at that time, and we said to each other that we were going to have a grand time that winter. There would be no more corporeal punishment, and we were going to be ruled by love.

The new teacher was a lady, and she opened the school with prayer. We hadn't seen it done before, and we were impressed, especially when she prayed that she might have grace and strength to rule the school with love. The school went on for several weeks, and we saw no rattan.

I was one of the first to break the rules of the school. The teacher asked me to stay behind. I thought the cane was coming out again, and I was in a fighting mood. She took me alone. She sat down and began

to talk to me kindly. That was worse than the cane;
I did not like it. She said:

"I have made up my mind that if I cannot control
the school by love, I will give it up. I will have no punishment. If you love me, try to keep the rules of the
school."

I felt something right here in my throat, and never
gave her any more trouble. She just put me under
grace. And that is what God does. God is love, and
He wants us all to love Him.

Free or Not Free?

When Miss Smiley went down South to teach, she
went to a hotel and found everything covered with dirt.
The tables were dirty, dishes dirty, beds were dirty. She
called an old colored woman who was in the house, and
said:

"Now, you know that the Northern people set you at
liberty. I came from the North, and I don't like dirt;
so I want you to clean the house."

The old colored woman set to work, and it seemed
as if she did more work in that half day than she had
done in a month before. When the lady got back the
colored woman came to her and said:

"Now, is I free or ben't I not? When I go to my old
massa he says I ain't free, and when I go to my own
people they say I is, and I don't know whether I'se free
or not. Some people told me Abraham Lincoln signed
a proclamation, but massa says he didn't; he hadn't any
right to."

So Christian people go along, not knowing whether
they are free or not. When they have been born of the
Spirit they are as free as air. Christ came for that

purpose, to free us from the guilt and power of sin. He didn't come to set us free and then leave us in servitude. He came to give us liberty now and forever.

The Haughty Infidel's Challenge

In the town of Hanover, in Germany, I am told that there is buried a German countess who denied the existence of God and ridiculed the idea of the resurrection. To show her contempt for Christianity she ordered that on her death her grave should be built of solid masonry and covered by large stones bound together by iron clamps. On this tomb was engraved her defiant challenge that through eternity this tomb should never be disturbed.

One day a seed from some tree, either blown by the wind or carried by a bird, became lodged in a small crevice of the tomb, where soon it sprouted and began to grow. And then, as if Nature mocked the haughty infidel, she quietly extended the delicate roots of that seedling under the massive blocks of stone and slowly raised them from their place. Although scarce four generations are passed since that tomb was sealed, that most insignificant seedling has accomplished what God Himself was challenged to accomplish.

Short-lived Esteem

Seventeen years ago I was in Paris at the time of the Great Exhibition. Napoleon the Third was then in his glory. Cheer after cheer would rise up as he drove along the streets of the city. A few short years and he fell from his lofty estate. He died an exile from his country and his throne, and where is his name to-day? Very few think about him at all, and if his name is mentioned it is not with love and esteem.

How empty and short-lived are the glory and the pride of this world! If we are wise we will live for God and eternity; we will get outside of ourselves, and will care nothing for the honor and glory of this world.

God is Not Dead

The story is told that Frederick Douglass, the great slave orator, once said in a mournful speech when things looked dark for his race:

"The white man is against us, governments are against us, the spirit of the times is against us. I see no hope for the colored race. I am full of sadness."

Just then a poor old colored woman rose in the audience, and said:

"Frederick, is God dead?"

Now, many a young believer is discouraged and disheartened when he realizes this warfare. He begins to think that God has forsaken him, that Christianity is not all that it professes to be. But he should rather regard it as an encouraging sign. No sooner has a soul escaped from his snare than the great Adversary takes steps to ensnare it again. He puts forth all his powers to recapture his lost prey. The fiercest attacks are made on the strongest forts, and the fiercer the battle the young believer is called on to wage, the surer evidence it is of the work of the Holy Spirit in his heart. God will not desert him in his time of need.

It Cost Him His Soul

"What is the value of this estate?" said a gentleman to another, as they passed a fine mansion surrounded by fair and fertile fields.

her house, and I went to see him. I found him in a rocking-chair, with that vacant, idiotic look upon him. Whenever he saw me he pointed at me and said: "Young man, seek first the kingdom of God." Reason was gone, but the text was there.

The Swan and the Crane

There is an old legend of a swan and a crane. A beautiful swan alighted by the banks of the water in which a crane was wading about seeking snails. For a few moments the crane viewed the swan in stupid wonder and then inquired:

"Where do you come from?"

"I come from heaven!" replied the swan.

"And where is heaven?" asked the crane.

"Heaven!" said the swan, "Heaven! have you never heard of heaven?" And the beautiful bird went on to describe the grandeur of the Eternal City. She told of streets of gold, and the gates and walls made of precious stones; of the river of life, pure as crystal, upon whose banks is the tree whose leaves shall be for the healing of the nations. In eloquent terms the swan sought to describe the hosts who live in the other world, but without arousing the slightest interest on the part of the crane.

Finally the crane asked: "Are there any snails there?"

"Snails!" repeated the swan; "no! Of course there are not."

"Then," said the crane, as it continued its search along the slimy banks of the pool, "you can have your heaven. I want snails!"

This fable has a deep truth underlying it. How many

a young person to whom God has granted the advantages of a Christian home, has turned his back upon it and searched for snails! How many a man will sacrifice his wife, his family, his all, for the snails of sin! How many a girl has deliberately turned from the love of parents and home to learn too late that heaven has been forfeited for snails!

TOPICAL INDEX

Ambitions, 112
Appropriation of Christ, 70
Ashamed of Jesus, 15
Aspiration, 105
Assurance, 63, 102
Atonement, 78, 94

Bible, 13, 97
Blamelessness, 17
Bondage, 48
Born of the Spirit, 22
Brotherly Love, 82

Children for Christ, 76
Choice, 24, 125
Christ, the World's Need, 35
Clean Heart, A, 81
Clear Vision, 95
Confessing Christ, 32, 36, 64, 75, 81, 106, 110
Confidence, 43
Constancy, 52
Conversion, 31
Conviction, 27, 123
Covetousness, 12

Dancing, 52
Death, 8, 22
Debts, 37
Deliverance, 106

Encouragement, 100
Enthusiasm, 41, 65
Eternal Life, 95
Example, 29
Excuses, 107

Faith, 9, 29, 39, 45, 68, 97
False Hopes, 88
Feelings, 40
Follow Jesus, 48
Forgiveness, 91
Full Surrender, 67

God, 87; First, 123; His Love, 54; Not Dead, 122; Love of, 67; Omnipresence of, 60; Omniscience of, 102
Grace, 75, 89, 101, 109, 110, 111, 119
Gratitude, 76
Growth, 51
Grumbling, 103
Guidance, 72

Habit, 67
Heart-searching, 114
Heaven, 98, 109
Holy Ghost, 113
Human Heart, The, 69
Humility, 15, 79, 92
Hypocrites, 102

Incentive for Work, 53
Infidelity, 69, 83
Insincerity, 105

Jealousy, 44, 72
Justification, 115

Kindness, 10, 59
Knowing the Bible, 66

Liberty, 120
Light-Bearing, 44
Looking Upward, 51
Love, 13, 50, 53, 71, 87, 89
Lying, 75

Nature Insufficient, 98
Need Supplied, 100

Obedience, 43, 58, 106

Pardon, 45
Peace, 104
Persecution, 8
Perseverence, 84, 98
Personal Application, 35
Praise, 7, 9
Prayer, 10, 29, 39, 54, 61, 74
Procrastination, 57, 77
Promises, 115
Prophecy Fulfilled, 17

Recognition in Heaven, 60
Redemption, 93
Regeneration, 15
Rest from Sin, 14
Restitution, 49
Resurrection, 16, 34, 108, 121

Sabbath-Keeping, 54
Salvation, 21, 28, 62, 77, 84, 88, 99, 105
Second Coming of Christ, 96
Sin, 31, 71, 81, 91, 113
Sins Blotted Out, 82
Small Sins, 47
Soul, Value of, 122
Soul-Winning, 104
Sowing and Reaping, 114, 116
Submission, 70
Surrender, 38

Temptation, 20, 80
Thanksgiving, 56
Thirst, 37
Trifling with Sin, 57
Trust, 32, 40, 117
Truth, 96

Unpardonable Sin, 80

Warning, 21, 115
Witnessing, 117
Worldliness, 83, 121